MW00607515

Gun Trader's GUIDE TO COLLECTIBLE KNIVES

Gun Trader's GUIDE TO COLLECTIBLE KNIVES

A Comprehensive, Fully Illustrated Reference with Current Market Values

MIKE ROBUCK

SKYHORSE PUBLISHING

Copyright © 2014 by Mike Robuck

All rights reserved. No part of this book may be reproduced in any manner without the express written consent of the publisher, except in the case of brief excerpts in critical reviews or articles. All inquiries should be addressed to Skyhorse Publishing, 307 West 36th Street, 11th Floor, New York, NY 10018.

Skyhorse Publishing books may be purchased in bulk at special discounts for sales promotion, corporate gifts, fund-raising, or educational purposes. Special editions can also be created to specifications. For details, contact the Special Sales Department, Skyhorse Publishing, 307 West 36th Street, 11th Floor, New York, NY 10018 or info@skyhorsepublishing.com.

Skyhorse® and Skyhorse Publishing® are registered trademarks of Skyhorse Publishing, Inc.®, a Delaware corporation.

Visit our website at www.skyhorsepublishing.com.

10 9 8 7 6 5 4 3 2 1

Library of Congress Cataloging-in-Publication Data is available on file.

Cover design by Owen Corrigan
Cover photo credit Mike Robuck and Thinkstock

ISBN: 978-1-62914-183-1
Ebook ISBN: 978-1-62914-320-0

Printed in China

CONTENTS

To my wife, Debbie, who is from the East Coast and did not grow up around knives. To her, passionately pursuing knives was probably akin to someone starting a wood screw collection, but she has endured.

Introduction

My interest in knife collecting was piqued by a knife show that aired on Friday nights many years ago. Being married, I had plenty of time to delve into the outer realm of cable TV land, which is where I came across the self-proclaimed "hoppin' mad hillbilly" knife show and his "killer car crusher knife deals of the day." (Which is not to be confused with the tactical knife shows that featured more than 300 knives for $14.99 plus shipping, although it might be worth your while to search "knife show katana accident" on YouTube.)

While the knives on that show weren't exactly top-shelf, they did trigger my memories of the traditional pocketknives I grew up with and carried. From there, I started buying knives off of eBay.

I tried to improve my chances on eBay by having two Internet browsers open at the same time on a dial-up connection in an attempt to bid on a knife auction faster than the competition. Cursing, gnashing of the teeth, pounding on the keyboard, pulling out what was left of my hair, and the occasional war-whoop of victory often followed the close of each auction.

I didn't know the difference between a knife that was made that year or thirty years ago, but that didn't stop me from bidding in the beginning.

After another frenzied round of bidding on eBay for what I thought was a rare and high-quality knife, I would often see the same knife sell for less a few days later.

Aside from the adrenaline surge of bidding on eBay, knife collecting also made me into a postal junkie of sorts as I waited on the postal worker to bring me a knife package.

After ripping open the package, more often than not I would be disappointed to receive a knife that didn't look anything like the one I bid on or came with an assortment of problems, including loose blades, cracked handles, and flat-out counterfeits.

I needed to up my game if I was going to keep collecting knives, so I started looking for local knife shows.

After months of corresponding with fellow knife enthusiasts through email and on Internet forums, I finally attended my first knife show, which was actually collocated in a much larger gun show at a Holiday Inn outside of Denver.

I was particularly looking forward to meeting an online buddy who had a friend selling traditional knives at the show. The knife dealer looked like an accountant by day except for the orange Harley-Davidson bandana on his head.

My friend, several other new enthusiasts, and I proceeded to pull out our knives in front of the dealer's booth prior to gossiping about them. At some point, we started setting them down on his table next to the knives he had for sale. After realizing that we were slowing draining the oxygen from in front of his booth, the Harley accountant scooped up our knives and put them underneath his table while we were giddily examining someone else's knife.

We had to ask for our knives back; then we were asked to move along if we weren't going to buy anything.

The long-winded point is that I had no clue what I was doing when I first started collecting knives.

There are several good knife books that are already in print, but one of my goals with this book is to impart the tips, lessons learned, and common sense that others took the time to teach me. If ignorance is truly bliss, I should have been a lot happier in the early days of my knife collecting, but mostly I just felt like a rube. Hopefully this book will be of value to new collectors and contain a few new kernels of information for those who have been at it for a while.

Mike Robuck
Grand Junction, Colorado
April 17, 2014

I: How to Collect Vintage Knives

*I*n the not-so-distant past, pocketknives were as ubiquitous as cell phones and apps. Maybe your father or grandfather carried a pocketknife and used it to cut off a plug of tobacco, or perhaps your first knife was a stockman pattern made by a company that is no longer in existence.

Vintage knives come in all shapes and sizes, from elegant pearl lobster patterns to fixed blades that saw service in both World Wars. Deciding what to collect and how to assemble a collection is the first order of business if you are new to the hobby.

On the East Coast, the Blade Show reigns supreme for knife collecting enthusiasts, while the Oregon Knife Show in Eugene has the largest assortment of vintage knives available at any show for purchase from the sellers' tables.

Keep in mind that if you're waiting in line to get into the Blade Show or Oregon Knife Show, other collectors are getting the first look at what's available via table holder badges or paid memberships.

The Blade Show in Atlanta runs for three days in late May or early June. Attendees can purchase VIP passes for the entire three days so they don't have to wait in line to buy day passes. Even better is to get a table holder badge from someone that has paid for a table on the show floor, which will allow you to enter the show floor before it officially opens each day. The Blade Show also offers "early bird" tickets on Friday, which will get attendees in two hours earlier than general admission tickets.

In a similar vein, attendees at the Oregon Knife Show can join the Oregon Knife Association in order to attend a members-only day on the Friday before the doors open up to the public.

There are also numerous small knife shows across the country, particularly in the South. Gun shows can also be a good source for finding vintage knives.

Lastly, check to see if there's a knife collectors club in your area. In addition to hosting their own shows or knife swaps, some knife club members possess a great deal of knowledge on knife collecting and are usually amiable to passing that information on.

What to Collect?

Some vintage knife companies, such as Case, have large national followings when it comes to collectors, but there were also regional knife companies that made high-quality knives for short periods of time.

A good starting point could be to pick a knife company that's from your state or maybe the same manufacturer that your grandfather carried every day. Some collectors focus only on a specific pattern or knives from a certain era.

Also muddying the waters a bit is the fact that some knife companies made contract knives for other companies or hardware stores. For example, Napanoch made knives for the Wilbert Cutlery Company, Hibbard, Spencer & Bartlett, and Will Roll Bearing, among others.

One of the more well-known premium knife giveaways in collectors' circles was the subscription premiums that *Hunter-Trader-Trapper* (*HTT*) offered.

Outdoorsman Arthur Robert Harding published the first issue of *HTT* in October of 1900, and the magazine continued into the latter part of the 1930s.

While *HTT* offered a variety of fixed blades and pocketknives over the years to entice readers into subscribing to the magazine, perhaps the best-known was the two-blade Remington Bullet trapper. For $2.50, an outdoorsman would get a year's subscription to the magazine and an R293 trapper, which was 5⅜" closed. For $2, *HTT* would send a friend a Christmas card, a smaller two-bladed trapper, and the yearly subscription.

The Bullet *HTT* with jigged bone was later replicated by other cutlery companies, as well as by custom knife makers, such as Tony Bose.

In 1925, *HTT* served up a harness jack with a large clip blade, acorn shield, grooved bolsters, and jigged bone in exchange for a new yearly $2 subscription. In this instance, the premium knife, which was pattern R373, was identical to the one in the Remington catalog, although the *HTT* ad cautioned that it had only a limited supply on hand.

It would appear that some of the subscription premium knives from *HTT* were one offs, meaning they were only available for one year. In the

"*Merry Christmas*"

WOULDN'T that old pal of yours thrill to receive a handsome Christmas card from us, telling him that we were sending him a year's subscription to Hunter-Trader-Trapper with your compliments? And wouldn't you thrill to receive one of the wonderful knives shown on this page, simply for sending your friend a year's subscription?

WE'LL SEND THE CARD

THE same day your order is received your knife is sent to you. There's no waiting or delay. We also address an envelope containing a handsome Christmas card to your friend—this card simply reads—"Season's Greetings—We are entering your name on our subscription list to receive Hunter-Trader-Trapper for one year with the compliments of (*Your name is filled in this space.*)" But we don't mail this greeting until about December 15th, so that it will arrive just before Christmas. The subscription will start with January, 1930 issue and your friend's first copy should arrive at approximately the same time as the card. It certainly will be a pleasant surprise to him. Of course, if you do not want him to know who is sending the magazine as a present, no Christmas card will be sent. The coupon below explains this part of it. Remember your knife will be sent immediately, so don't put off ordering.

Send In TODAY

A GIFT THAT IS APPRECIATED

Many people believe that a subscription to H-T-T is not a gift that is appreciated by the receiver but they are badly mistaken. A subscription comes to him every month and reminds him of your friendship twelve times and not only once. It isn't a gift that is used or worn out in a few weeks and discarded. We received hundreds of Christmas subscriptions last year and we received letters from many of these new subscribers, telling us how much they appreciated receiving H-T-T. You will make no mistake in selecting H-T-T for your outdoor pals.

$**2**.00

Subc. price including Knife R-272S

Select Your Knife

BOTH these knives are genuine Remingtons, made especially for us. The design has the approval of hunters, trappers and outdoor men everywhere. The handles are seasoned bone stag, linings are brass, steel is the best that can be made. The springs are flexible, allowing the blades to be easily opened. Illustrations are actual size. Measure them. The "little" fellow at the right has three inch blades and will answer the needs of most everyone. The big boy has four inch blades and is a nice handful of useful steel. It will equal a sheath knife in many respects.

For only $2.00 we will enter your pal's subscription and will send you knife No. R-272S, postage prepaid.

If you want the large knife, No. R-293, your remittance must be $2.50. We pay the postage.

Get that knife you've been needing, and make that pal of yours happy this Christmas. Send in right now. You'll not regret it when you see your knife, and the satisfaction you get from making the other fellow happy can't be measured in dollars and cents.

HUNTER-TRADER-TRAPPER
Columbus, ∴ ∴ ∴ Ohio, U. S. A.

$**2**.50

Subscription price including Knife R-293

HUNTER-TRADER-TRAPPER, Columbus, Ohio, U. S. A.

Here is $............. covering the cost of the following.

Send H-T-T for one year to this address:
(Also send Christmas card bearing my name)

Send Knife No. .... to me at the address below.

....

....

....

NOTE—In case you do not want your friend to know who is sending him the magazine as a present, simply draw a line through the words on the above coupon. (Also send Christmas card bearing my name.)

for hunting—
for trapping—
for all purposes—

No. 373

Illustration Natural Size

A Genuine Remington Knife for One New Subscription

THE steel in the blades of this knife is the same as that used in the highest priced Remington—it is the best obtainable. The large clip blade is strong and has a keen durable cutting edge. The punch or reamer blade has many practical uses around the camp or on the trap line especially recommended for punching holes in leather or scraping. It can be resharpened on any good whet-stone-a most desirable feature.

THE handles are American Bone Stag—properly cured, seasoned and toughened. They fit snugly and accurately. You can get a good grip on this knife. Bolsters are of polished nickel silver and knife is full brass lined.

THIS knife is of solid construction throughout and is built to stand the requirements of hunters or campers. Truly it is a handful of useful steel and a value which you seldom find. None sold separately. Only a limited supply on hand. Better order immediately. This knife given free for one new yearly subscriber to H-T-T at $2.00.

HUNTER-TRADER-TRAPPER
Columbus, Ohio

Here is $2.00. Please send your magazine for one year to

Send knife No. 373 to_____

◄◄Use the Coupon

It is easy to get a new subscription to Hunter-Trader-Trapper. Simply show a few of your old copies to some of your friends and it is certain that one or more of them will subscribe.

HUNTER-TRADER-TRAPPER
Columbus, Ohio, U. S .A.

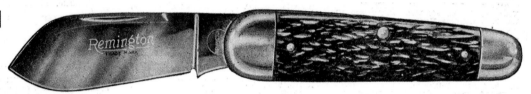

REMINGTON (BULLDOG) KNIFE

Better hurry on this one. We bought all of these Remington had and can't get any more. Get yours now before it's too late. Brass lined, nickel silver bolsters, bone stag handle. Only one blade, but what a blade it is. You can sharpen a pencil or take the lid off a box and still have a knife left. With only one early subscription at____ **$1.50**

Write your name and address in the margin below and return with remittance direct to

Hunter-Trader-Trapper, 386 So. 4th St., Columbus, Ohio, U. S. A.

October 1936 issue, *HTT* dangled a single-blade Remington Bulldog in jigged bone that used the same frame as the company's jumbo jack sleeve-board pattern, which had three blades. Unlike the regular Remington product line, the Bulldog didn't have a pattern number or company name on the blade tang, although it did feature a blade etch.

The early subscription premium cost of the Bulldog was $1.50 a year, which was 30 cents fewer than the newsstand price. At 3½" closed, Bulldog owners could "sharpen a pencil or take the lid off of a box and still have a knife left."

Due to the interest in Remington knives by collectors, the limited availability, and perhaps a low survival rate, the *HTT* knives are highly collectible.

Finding which company made contract knives for other companies can be a nice subset of knife collecting. There are lots of searches on eBay for Napanoch, but not that many for Will Roll Bearing. They're the same knife with a different name, but the latter usually costs less.

Other subsets of collecting areas include regional or national hardware store brands, advertisers' brands (where an advertiser's name is etched on a blade or present on the scales), and retailers' brands (such as local banks or sporting good stores). Some military knives and early fixed blades are also highly collectible with prices to match in some instances.

The bottom line? Collect what you like. As you learn more about knives, your tastes may evolve to other areas, patterns, or companies.

▲ These two-blade advertising penknives by George Ibberson & Company have metal, plastic, and ivory scales. The knives are 3¼" closed and date to the 1930s.

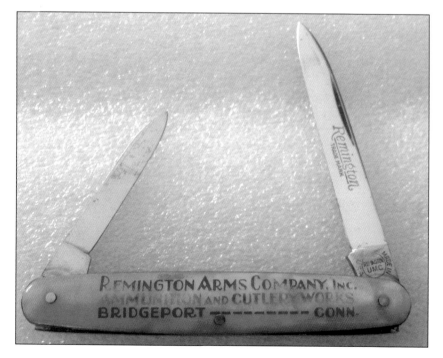

◀ Remington advertised its brand on a two-blade penknife.

Knives as an Investment

There's a perception among some collectors, especially in the current economy, that their knife collections are an investment that will make up for the demise of their 401ks. There are a small percentage of dealers and collectors who are able to buy and flip knives for a profit, but for the most part the rest of us are better off buying and collecting knives because we enjoy them.

Recent knives that were made as collectibles, commemoratives, and limited editions generally don't fare well value-wise over the long term. While a buyer is trying to keep up with the latest special edition trapper, chances are the first one he or she bought five years ago has gone down in value by as much as 50 percent because other collectors want the latest special edition.

Trends come and go in any hobby. What was red-hot a few years ago may be in the bargain bin at the next knife show you attend. The bottom line for buying knives is to buy what you like.

Taking Care of Your Knives

Taking proper care of your knives should be near the top of your priority list. Don't be the guy or gal that throws them into a desk drawer or puts them all in a shoebox to rattle around against each other.

Padded knife rolls with Velcro fold-over tops are one option for storing a number of knives. Large leather-type knife rolls can hold a large number of knives, but eventually the elastic bands that hold the knives in place lose their elasticity. For those high-end knives, padded pouches are the way to go even though they cost more.

Sheffield knife companies put "oil the joint" on blades for a reason. On a traditional folding knife, oil keeps the blade tang and backspring from grinding against each other. Light gun oil or mineral oil work well because they're not heavy, gunky oils. Avoid other oils, such as motor oil, olive oil, peanut oil, and WD-40.

For wood, bone, and stag scales, use either mineral oil, which can be found in the pharmacy section of a grocery store, or lemon furniture oil. Lemon furniture oil was designed to penetrate wood, and it puts a nice luster on natural scale materials and has a pleasant smell to it. Mineral oil is a good all-around oil to use on the blades, joints, and scales.

If you have early vintage celluloid knives, store them away from the rest of your collection. The outgassing of celluloid scales can cause corrosion on knives that are stored near them.

Also, it's a good idea to store fixed-blade sheaths separately from the knives and out of sunlight and extreme heat. Use leather care products, such as Pecard Leather Dressing, on the sheaths so they don't dry out and crack.

Periodically taking out your collection for cleaning is not only a useful ritual, but it is also a good way to enjoy your knives.

Clean out the inside of a vintage pocketknife, which is where lint and black gunk sometimes reside, with oil and a toothpick with a piece of paper towel on the end. Also make sure the joints are clean of lint or other debris.

If the blades have light rust spots, oil them and use a toothpick or Popsicle stick to try to remove the rust after a few days. If you absolutely feel as though you can't live with a little rust or black pepper spots on the metal parts of a knife, use steel wool or a very fine grit of sandpaper, but go easy. In general, the heavy cleaning of any knife reduces its value.

Buying Online

Not everyone can make it to a knife show or join a local knife club. Obviously eBay has changed the dynamics of many hobbies by bringing collectors and sellers together across vast distances, but at the same time, it has created a void with the lack of personal interactions between the two.

Some sellers of fake knives on eBay rely on blurred pictures and terms such as "barn finds", "factory finds", and "mint" in their auctions. Be wary of knives that have pictures taken at odd angles. If the seller doesn't provide an inspection period whereby you can return the knife in a given time frame, ask for one. If a seller isn't willing to take better pictures or provide an inspection period, move on.

If you're attempting to buy a knife on eBay, ask questions if you're not sure. Also ask for better pictures, including pictures that are in focus. For instance, ask for a picture of the blade nestled down in the closed position to see if it's too short for the frame that it's in. Ask for close-up pictures of the tang stamp and pins, the latter of which could have hard-to-see cracks around them.

Take a pass on sellers who aren't interested in answering questions or taking specific pictures for you. No matter how high a fever you have for a particular knife on eBay, keep in mind that almost invariably another one will turn up somewhere, probably after you've just purchased another expensive knife that has blown your budget.

And lastly, don't be fooled by sellers that have 100 percent positive feedback on eBay. The feedback ratings on eBay generally aren't worth the paper they are printed on. Some known eBay counterfeiters seem to be the nicest folks in the world, and they will happily return your money for a bogus knife before banning you from future auctions and then re-listing said knife again. Check a seller's history in regard to what he or she has bought off of eBay; run away if they have bought boxes of knife parts.

EBay can also be a resource for gauging what a knife is worth at a given time. A search of completed auctions will give you the final winning bid, but a more accurate determination of the value might be from the third-highest bidder, because the top-two bidders could have gone to the mat for it, according to knife expert Bernard Levine.

Looking at completed auctions will also give you an idea of what type of knives a seller has offered in the past. See a bunch of fakes? Run, don't walk to the next seller.

Some sellers of online knife auctions employ shill bidders to artificially drive up the price on a knife. Shill bidders typically bid up the price at the beginning or middle of an auction, then drop out during the final days, hours, or minutes.

There are reputable knife dealers online, both within eBay and on various individual web sites. Ask around.

Do your research, ask the sellers questions, ask an expert; then bid or pass. In order to stave off buyer's remorse, determine ahead of time what the knife is worth to you and how much you are willing to spend.

II: Counterfeit Knives: The Kudzu of Knife Collecting

With highly sought-after patterns from companies such as Remington, Case, and Winchester going for thousands of dollars, it's little wonder that counterfeit knives continue to crop up like mushrooms after a hard rain.

A Marbles hunting knife from the 1920s was made to be used and used hard. For that reason alone, it's hard to find very many pristine examples of some patterns because people back in the day looked at knives as everyday tools that were bought to perform specific or day-to-day tasks.

Vintage, mint pocketknives or fixed-blade knives are rare and can go for high dollar amounts, which means that there are plenty of counterfeits on the market. Even veteran collectors can be fooled by fake, reworked, or counterfeit knives. Some collectors who suffer from a bit of hubris refuse to believe that they've bought a fake knife for a lot of money, and the counterfeit eventually makes its way into another set of hands.

If you collect knives for very long, it's almost inevitable that you will acquire a counterfeit at some point. Counterfeit knives come in various flavors, including a Frankenknife built out of miscellaneous knife parts, a knife built from leftover factory knife parts, a knife with new blades welded to the tangs, and a fantasy knife not made by actual cutlery companies.

Old Names, New Knives

Also be aware that there are thousands of knives with vintage cutlery names on the tangs that are actually modern knives. Over the years, various entities have bought up the rights to the old company names. For new collectors, it's disappointing to find out a Holley knife was recently made in Germany instead of Lakeville, Connecticut.

Entire books, such as Gerald Witcher's *Counterfeiting Antique Cutlery*, have been written on fake knives. On one end of the spectrum, the lengths and depths that the best counterfeiters will go to fool the knife-buying public show instances of actual talent, but the other end is chock full of poorly made knockoffs that should alert you at first glance.

The axiom knowledge is power especially rings true when it comes to identifying counterfeit or reworked knives. Buying reprints of vintage knife catalogs—get the ones that have the actual sizes of the knives in them—can help you see what a particular knife is

▶ There are numerous issues with these two attempts at Remington knives, including the wrong type and color of bone jigging, sloppy shield mounts, and cold-stamped names on the tangs.

▲ Hitler or Nazi pocket knives fall under the realm of fantasy knives since they were made in the United States.

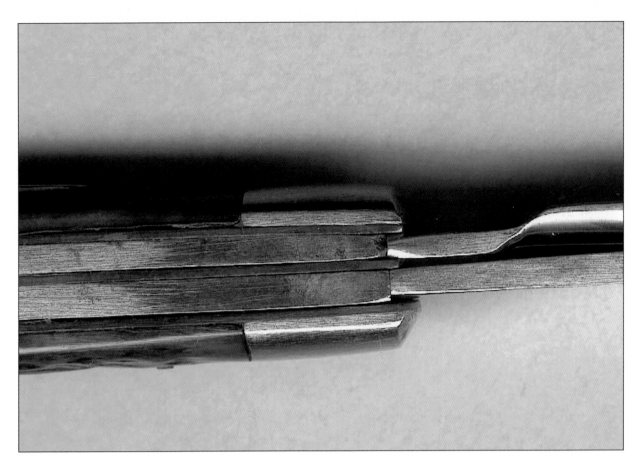

▲ The manner in which these blades do not line up with the back springs should raise red flags even for beginning collectors.

supposed to look like, but the best indicator of all in regard to whether a knife is legitimate or not is to examine it in hand.

If you're really serious about your knife collecting endeavors, the grad school version is to examine all sorts of knives up close and personal and even take some apart. Why should you closely examine kitchen knives at the antique store when you're a bowie knife collector? Because there just might come a day when someone offers you a bowie knife with a stag handle from a carving set.

Knife Buying: Up Close and Personal

Whenever you are inspecting a knife in person, examine it closely. Sounds simple, but often buyers will open the blades, examine the tang stamps, and pull out their wallets. Really focus on the swedges, pins, bolsters, the inside of a knife, blade grinds, nail pulls, springs, liners, tangs, kicks, sheaths, and handle materials.

While you're closely examining a knife, either by pictures on eBay or in person, ignore the story that the seller is spinning to go with it. Yarns are for campfires and grandkids.

Guidelines: What to Look For

What follows are some guidelines that will, hopefully, help beginners avoid fakes and scams:

- Is the tang stamp or other metal parts of the knife darker than the rest of the blade? Then the blade has been buffed, but the buffing wheel couldn't reach other areas, or the seller didn't think to buff other parts of the knife. A knife that is supposed to be seventy years old should show its age, and the wear should be even across the knife. Even mint knives will have some pepper spots.
- Aside from the shiny brightness, wavy lines on blades can also indicate buffing. Some buyers like their old knives to look new, but if a vintage knife has buffed blades, bolsters, and springs and the seller calls it mint, keep moving.
- While some vintage knives have been altered to look minty fresh, the opposite is also true when

acids are used to make a new knife look old. For the most part, the patina on knives forms uniformly. If a knife blade looks like it has been dipped in a liquid to give it that old-timey look, it may have.

- Check the font on the tang stamp. Modern fonts look different than those used at the turn of the century up to World War II. Learn the what the old fonts look like.

- Blade tangs are stamped, not engraved. Some sellers will file down a less-desirable name on an old knife and cold stamp a more collectible company name on the tang. Since these stamps are applied after a knife has been heat treated at a factory, cold stamping causes slight curls to rise up around the letters of the name.

- Is the jigging correct for that brand of knife or period? Over the past few years, older knives with newer-style jigging have been cropping up. The new jigging looks great, but it's like putting a spoiler on a Model T.

- Vintage knives have pinned shields. Most recent knives have glued shields. Look on the inside of a knife with a flashlight to see if you can spot the shield pin.

- Everyone wants to score a great knife at a low price, but take a deep breath before buying a knife that looks too good to be true. And on the obverse, a poorly made knife with a well-known name on the tang is really just a poorly made knife.

- Knives with spun pins were generally made before World War I. All the pins on a knife should have the same color and shape. It's a red flag if a pin is missing, if the hole is larger than the pin, or if the pin looks like it was hammered in with blunt force.

- If you're not sure, ask someone. There are knife experts that charge a nominal fee to evaluate knives on eBay or from sellers and dealers. There are also numerous online forums where counterfeit knives are discussed in length, but be aware that some of the forum responders are eBay sellers

▲ Cold stamping causes the letters to have slight curls around the edges. The font is also incorrect.

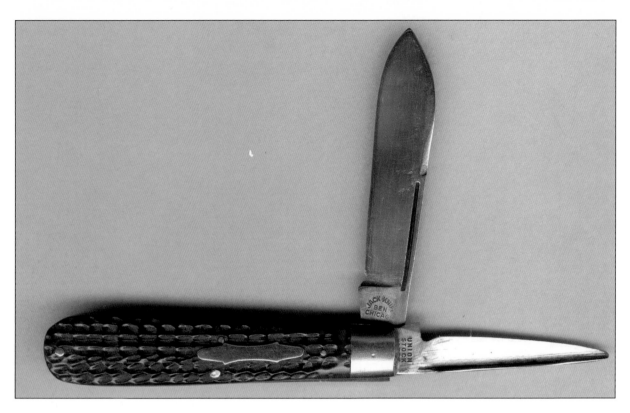

▲ The shield is surface mounted on this Jack Knife Ben counterfeit, and the jigged bone is recent.

themselves or not as knowledgeable as they may think. Actual knife clubs are also good resources for learning about knives, but until you know for certain, question everything.

Lastly, if you get hosed on buying a fake knife, do other members of the knife community a favor by not passing the counterfeit knife along to the next unsuspecting buyer as the real deal. It's tough to take a loss on a knife, but some collectors knowingly keep the bogus knives in their collections as reminders of their mistakes. They also make great gifts for people who don't collect knives but still need to cut things with a sharp edge.

III: Knife Show Etiquette

Attending a knife or gun show is a great opportunity to not only meet fellow enthusiasts but also to handle more knives in person. Shows are also good venues to ask questions en route to learning more about knives in general or about particular brands and patterns.

Proper knife show etiquette falls under the realm of common sense for the most part, but here are a few dos and don'ts to consider:

- Don't pick up a knife from a seller's table without first asking for permission. Sellers may be dealing with several customers at the same time, and it's hard for them to keep track of what everyone is doing. High-end knives have been known to go missing at shows. Asking first will put you in good graces with the seller.
- Don't open all of the blades on a pocketknife at the same time. Open them one at a time, and don't let them slam shut when closing them.
- Stick to your business and don't say something like "I saw one of those same knives for forty dollars less on an online site," when discussing terms with a dealer.
- Don't test how sharp a knife is by poking the tip on your finger or by sliding your finger along the blade edge. If that seems like plain old common sense, there's a reason some knife dealers keep a box of Band-Aids on their tables at shows.
- Don't be a brown bagger at a knife show. Brown baggers show up at knife shows to sell their own knives without paying for a table. If you're bringing along knives to trade, make sure you have permission from the seller behind the table to bring them out.
- If you're not going to buy something, move along. Sellers at knife shows are there to make money, not to have you block their tables while you and a friend discuss your latest eBay acquisition.
- Don't wipe the blades down after handling them. Let the seller clean them up.
- To avoid corrosion, keep your fingerprints off the blades of high-end collectors' knives.

And finally, deals can be had near the end of some knife shows, as the dealers would rather sell knives than pack them back up again. Instead of insulting a seller with a low-ball offer, try "What's the lowest you would take?" as an opening gambit.

The last day or final hours are also a good window for asking sellers for more detailed information about the knives they have for sale. Just remember to do so when the tables aren't crowded with prospective buyers.

◀ The Oregon Knife Show is one of the premier knife shows in the nation and features a wide range of traditional knives.

IV: Inside the Knife: Swedges

by Kerry Hampton

While there are several hallmarks of a well-made traditional pocketknife, one in particular is the use of swedges on the blades.

At its most basic level, a swedge is an unsharpened bevel cut along the top of a blade. While swage is the historically accurate name, the more common term used today is swedge. Swage is actually pronounced swedge, the latter of which rhymes with ledge. So there you have it.

Origins of Swedges

I believe swedge is a derivative of swage and comes from blacksmithing or bladesmithing. A swage block was used in the shaping of hot steel. The idea with bladesmithing was to get the piece being formed by hammering as close as possible to the final product before grinding. Swaging could have come from hammering the swages into the blades first. After that, they would be cleaned up by grinding, but not as much material would be wasted using this method. This could be how swages evolved into swedges.

According to traditional custom knife maker Tony Bose, there are four basic purposes for swedges. The first is the aesthetic appeal; some kitchen knives have long swedges along one side for eye appeal only. The second is that swedges make the blades thinner at the spine and improve their ability to cut. The third is really the brass tack of swedges, and that's making room for the blades to open and close without rubbing against each other. The fourth purpose is to provide access to nail pulls on knives.

Often working in conjunction with swedges, knife blades were crinked, which means they were slightly offset to help the blades pass each other when opening and closing them and fit alongside each other in the closed position. Knives without proper swedges and crinking develop rub marks on the blades.

"Back in the old days, if there was a swedge on a knife, it was there for a reason," said Bose. "Everything they did was for a reason, but as time passed, they started cutting corners by grinding the blades a little thinner and not doing the swedge. Some companies were still doing bold swedges into the '40s, but after

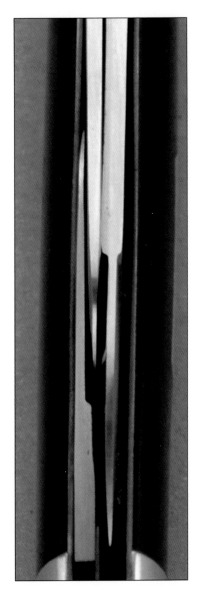

▲ This three-blade cattle knife by Empire features some good examples of swedge work. From the top you can see that there isn't a lot of extra room for the blades.

that they were mostly little draw swedges on there or a knockoff corner."

Types of Swedges

There are two types of swedges: cut swedge and drawn swedge. The cut swedge plunges in where it begins on the spine and tapers out toward the tip. A correct swedge will end before it gets to the tip of the

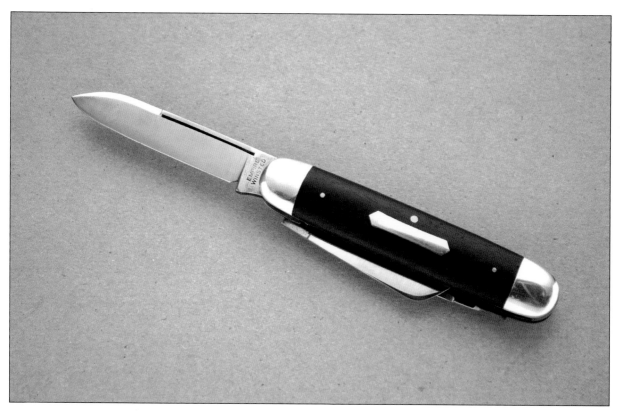

▲ The master spear blade has symmetrically cut swedges that taper out before the tip.

◀ The sheepsfoot blade features drawn swedges on both sides.

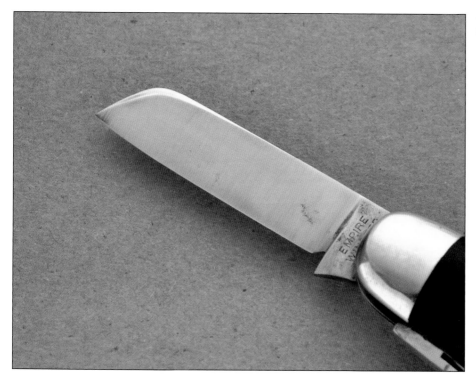

blade. Otherwise, blade sharpening over time could potentially involve the swedge, resulting in an ugly blade.

The drawn swedge starts gradually from where it begins on the spine and tapers out again toward the tip.

On multi bladed knives, such as the cattle knife shown here, the choice of which swedge to use was heavily influenced by the space that was needed for the blades to pass each other.

Cut swedges offered maximum clearance, which begins right at the plunge near the tang. Drawn swedges offer maximum clearance only at the center of the swedge. Those differences in position of clearance along the length of a particular blade generally determined which swedge was used.

Swedges took time and skill to implement. As the knife making process became more mechanized and industrialized, knife swedges started to disappear. The attention to detail on earlier knife swedges is just one example of the cutlery companies in general, and grinders in particular, being on top of their game.

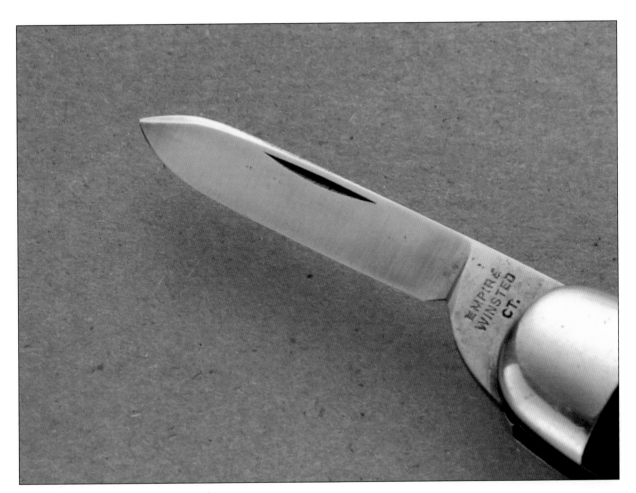

▲ One side of the pen blade has a drawn swedge.

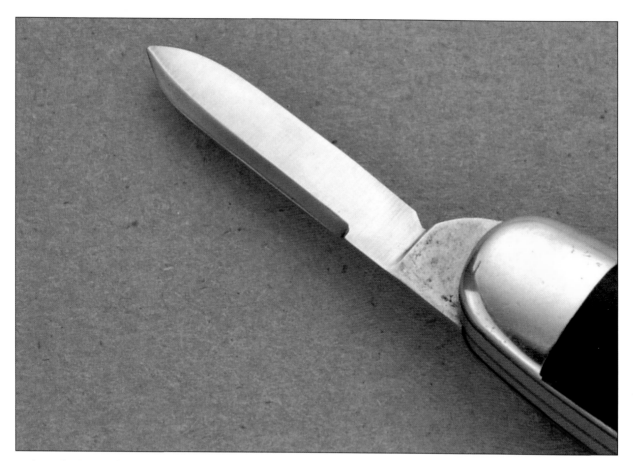

▲ The inside of the pen blade features a cut swedge to allow more room when it passes the blade next to it.

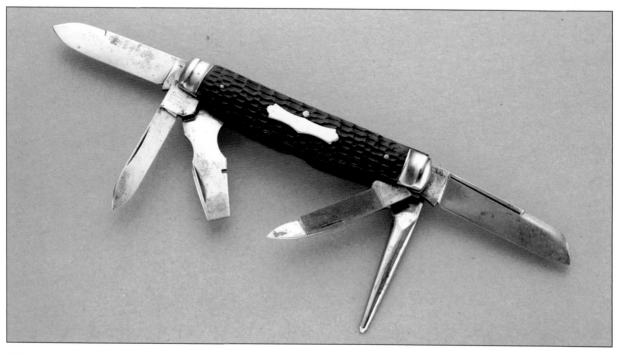

▲ The swedges on each blade play a part in making this six-blade Camillus knife work well. Eye appeal is also a factor in the use of swedges.

V: Outside the Knife: Jigged Bone

No one, it seems, knows exactly when jigged bone was first used as scales or handles on traditional pocket-knives and fixed blades.

Cattle shin bones were the medium of choice for jigging on knife handles, but it can also be seen on second cut stag, which is the inner part of a piece of stag after the rough bark exterior is sliced off. The jigging process added a textured finish to knife handles or scales, which not only improved the looks but also, in theory at least, improved the grip. In addition to jigged bone, there were also smooth bone scales and sawcut bone scales on barlows.

The general consensus is that the use of bone came about as a cheaper alternative to stag scales in England and Germany in the 1880s. Scratted or scored bone, which is done by hand and includes basic lines or geometric designs, started to appear in Sheffield, England on low-end knives in the late 18th century.

Early Patents

In Germany, a patent was granted in 1892 for a device that was used to hand-jig stag horn imitation scales made of "bone or other suitable material", according to German knife historian Henning Ritter.

According to recent research by N. Brian Huegel, two United States patents were issued in 1880 for bone jigging tools, with one also describing a dying process after the bone was jigged using three wood dyes. (Other methods of coloring bone included the use of potassium permanganate, which was also used on stag. Potassium permanganate actually burns the stag or bone, and too much of it can cause the handle material to become brittle and flake off. Today custom knife makers use an assortment of wood dyes, tea, and even a boiled onionskin broth to create the brown colors of bone.)

After the 1800s, jigged bone became prevalent in the United States as former employees of Sheffield and Solingen factories emigrated here and helped found new cutlery companies.

Knife companies often referred to jigged bone as imitation stag. Remington called its jigged bone stag, while real stag was genuine stag in its catalogs. Similarly Union Cutlery used the terms stag and natural stag in its catalogs.

Schrade Mechanizes Jigging

George Schrade began selling his patented jigging machine around 1925; prior to that, the jigging was

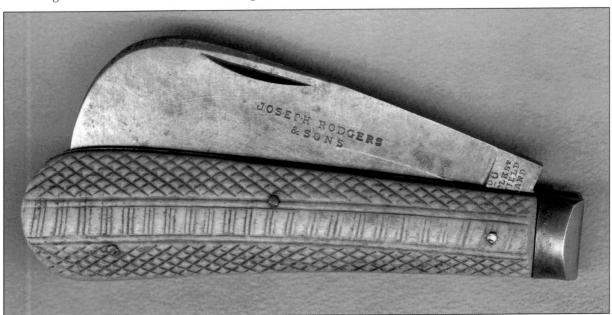

▲ The scratted scales on the Joseph Rodgers & Sons pruner were done with hand tools.

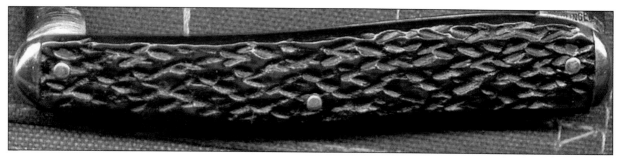

▲ Henckels called its jigged bone imitation stag bone.

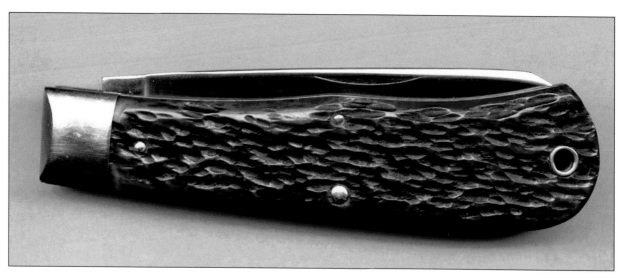

▲ Here's one example of the jigging that Remington used. Some knife companies had more than one jigging pattern, and often the size of the knife determined which pattern would be used.

done by hand. Schrade's machines could be set up to cut different jigging patterns, and Schrade was known for its peachseed jigging pattern. Schade's machines have been passed on to various knife companies over the years.

With current factory knives and collectors who buy them, there are a lot of different names for the various jigged bone patterns, but two of the known names used on vintage knives were Indian Trail, which is commonly referred to as worm groove today, and Rogers Stag, which is now referred to as Rogers bone by today's collectors. In a similar vein, some collectors refer to early Case bone as green bone although it's actually brown.

Over time, the top edges of jigged bone wear down from being in pockets or sheaths, and the color can also fade. Jigged bone in its unaltered state has crisp gouges, uniform colors, and often the jigging goes all the way out to the edges of the scales and up to the bolsters.

Be aware that there are a variety of imitation bone handle materials out there that closely resemble actual bone. There are some who advocate the hot pin test to see whether the handle material is actually bone or some sort of imitation material. Poking just about anything with a red-hot pin seems like a bad idea, but causing irrevocable damage to a knife's scales can be avoided. Instead, use a magnifying glass to look for the haversian canals, which look like pores, to determine if it is bone.

▲ Schrade's peachseed bone is popular among today's knife collectors.

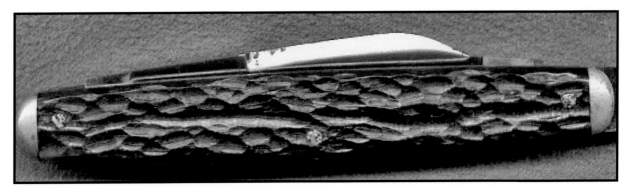

▲ Collectors today refer to this type of jigged bone as worm groove, but it's actual name is Indian Trail, which was used by Cattaraugus and other knife companies.

▲ Barlows often came with sawcut bone scales.

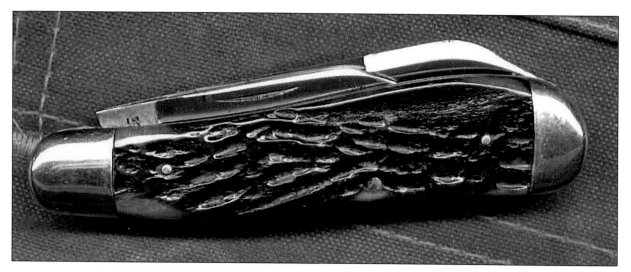

▲ This early Winchester knife might have Napanoch bone scales, which was a company that Winchester Arms acquired.

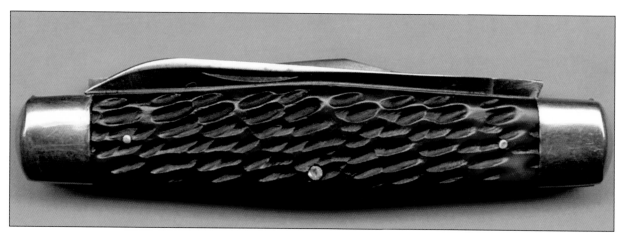

▲ The New York Knife Company is well known for its jigging pattern and distinctive shade of brown.

History: Rogers Bone

by Bernard Levine, originally appeared in *Knife World*

Rogers bone was made by the Rogers Manufacturing Company of Rockfall, Connecticut. To learn more about the company, I interviewed Vincent Bitel Sr., President of the Rogers Manufacturing Company, and his son, Vincent Bitel Jr.

The elder Bitel informed me that the firm started in business in 1891 making manufactured bone products and also bone fertilizer. It began to make jigged bone pocketknife scales around the turn of the century. Other manufactured bone products included combs, toothbrush handles, baby pacifiers, and one

of their biggest sellers, corncob pipe bits. This particular item was discontinued in the 1950s.

Early in the century, one of this firm's competitors in the bone business was Rogers & Hubbard. About the time of World War I, Rogers Mfg. Co. traded its bone fertilizer operation to Rogers & Hubbard and received in return the other firm's manufactured bone products business. From that time forward, Rogers Mfg. Co. was the nation's largest maker of manufactured bone products.

At first, all of the bone used by Rogers Mfg. Co. came from domestic cattle. By the 1920s, and perhaps even earlier, all of it was coming from overseas, mainly from Argentina.

Rogers Stag Then, Rogers Bone Now

Most of Rogers's pocketknife handle material was made in the distinctive jigging pattern that collectors call Rogers bone, but that the firm, in fact, called Rogers Stag. Rogers Stag was made using a specially designed jigging machine. The company also made small quantities of other styles of jigged bone for pocketknives.

Rogers Mfg. Co. also made jigged bone for hunting knives and kitchen utensils. For hunting knives, they made a style of jigging they called Indian Trail. This is a long random worm style of jigging. Their biggest customer for bone kitchen utensil handles was Landers, Frary & Clark, who used the bone mainly on kitchen forks.

During World War II, Rogers's production of jigged bone handles continued without interruption. Many of those handles wound up on cutlery items made for the government.

The bone used by Rogers during the war was all imported. It came from Argentina, Brazil, and a new source, Australia. The Australian bone came mainly from old (fifteen years or older) tough range cattle. This made it thick and dense and strong. This heavy Australian bone was used mainly for hunting knife handles.

In the 1950s, cost-conscious cutlery manufacturers began to discontinue the production of bone-handled pocketknives. Rogers Mfg. Co. changed with the times and began to offer synthetic pocketknife handles. The elder Bitel, who started with Rogers in 1955, was involved in the transition. He said that Rogers Mfg. Co. was the first firm to produce pocketknife scales made out of Delrin (a DuPont acetal resin). One trademark Rogers used for synthetic handle materials was Romco.

Rogers Mfg. Co. last sold bone pocketknife handle material in 1962. The firm still supplies limited quantities of synthetic handle material to the cutlery industry, but domestic and foreign competitors have taken most of that specialized business away.

History: Winterbottom Bone

By Bernard Levine, originally written for The National Knife Collectors Association

Some time ago, I received an interesting packet of information from Steve Deer of Indiana. He used to collect Queen Cutlery Co. knives, and one of the distinctive features of many Queens is their Winterbottom Bone handles, called genuine Frontier bone stag by Queen. He discovered that Winterbottom bone was made in Egg Harbor, New Jersey, at the eastern edge of the Pine Barrens.

The Egg Harbor Public Library put Deer in touch with Ivor Winterbottom, the oldest grandson of Samuel Winterbottom, founder of Winterbottom

▲ Rogers' Indian Trail jigged bone stretches across this Cattaraugus folding hunter knife.

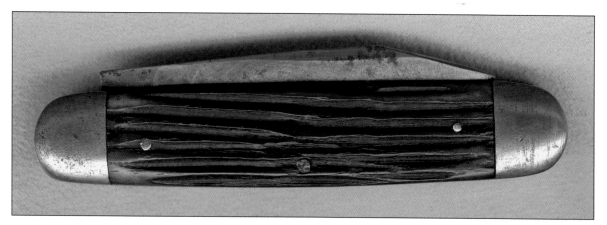

▲ This early W.R. Case & Sons Bradford knife sports red Winterbottom scales.

Cutlery Works, and the last Winterbottom to be connected with the firm. In the packet he sent me, Deer included an August 8, 1983 letter to him from Ivor Winterbottom. Some excerpts:

"A thumbnail history would start somewhere about 1885 when Samuel Winterbottom left Sheffield for Philadelphia, leaving his wife and three children behind. Sam's first job was peddling window glass in the streets and glazing windows. One of his fellow peddlers (supposedly) was Henry Disston, who was selling saws from a wheelbarrow. In later years they joined forces and made special circular saws for cutting bone. Some time before 1890, Samuel Winterbottom moved to Egg Harbor City, New Jersey, and sent for his family."

"In 1890 he set up his first shop . . . Winterbottom Carter. S.W. was the craftsman, Carter the deskman [bookkeeping]. As time passed, Samuel's four sons entered the business: Harry, Jack, Ernest, and Fred (born in the US)."

"When the US entered World War I, the factory began making handles for knives and bayonets. Carter, being of Quaker belief, would have nothing to do with war materials and left the company. Up to this time, most of the work was done by hand. Orders were so heavy the brothers designed and hand-built machines that kept 125 men working six days a week. After the war, the brothers continued to make handles from bone, wood, celluloid, and other materials for almost everyone in the cutlery industry. . . . Some of our customers I can remember were Schatt & Morgan (before 1920), Queen, Imperial, Camillus, Cattaraugus, and KA-BAR. There were 10 or 12 more, but I can't think of them right now."

▲ Camillus used a large jigging pattern on this 4⅛" closed equal-end jack knife.

"The first [bone] stag of the [Winterbottom] type came to life during this period. It was all done by hand, and I had many blisters to prove it. Fred decided we had to have a machine to do this job. As you know, every piece of real deer horn stag is different. To make a machine that would make different patterns was quite a chore."

"Finally it was made, and we thought we had the industry sewed up.

But some fellow smarter than we were bought up some knives with our handles, pulled off the handles, made molds, and cast [copies of] our handles in plastic. This, combined with US Department of Agriculture restrictions on foreign bone and a Brazilian embargo on rosewood made things so expensive that [our operation] could no longer survive. In 1968 I sold the business to one of our customers, who makes wood and plastic handles for their own use."

A biography of Samuel Winterbottom in the 1924 volume "*South Jersey: A History*" provides a little more accurate information on the early history of the Winterbottom family and firm.

"John Winterbottom, Mr. Winterbottom's father, was born and died in Sheffield, England, and was a bone-cutter by occupation, his trade linking his name with the world-famous cutlery manufacturers of that city. The family had followed similar lines of activity in England for 130 years. . . .

"Samuel Winterbottom was born in 1857 . . . and early in life became employed as a bone-cutter and manufacturer of handles of all kinds for knives in association with his father."

According to this book, Samuel worked in the paper industry in Philadelphia, Valley Forge, and Egg Harbor until 1891, when he set up in the handle and novelty business. He started with one employee. A year later he had four and moved to a larger building.

By 1924, Samuel Winterbottom had one hundred people on his company's payroll. Amber and tortoise-shell handles were a specialty. His eldest son, Harry, born in Sheffield in 1880, was then the firm's business manager. His second son, John, born in 1885, was factory superintendent. His third son, Ernest, born in 1886, and his youngest, Frederick, born in New Jersey in 1898, were both factory foremen.

VI: Glory Days: The Golden Age of US Cutlery

The manufacture of pocketknives and fixed-blade knives has a rich history in the United States, including the so-called Golden Age of cutlery that ran roughly from the turn of the century up to World War II.

The early cutlery companies that burst forth in a blaze of glory to serve the regional needs of their customers were numerous from the 1840s on, and some served as a microcosm of the evolution of the pocketknife manufacturing process. For example, most of the early knife companies in the United States were located near rivers in New England in order to harness the power of the flowing water to turn grinding wheels and power other equipment.

A Melting Pot of Influences

Due to restrictive tariffs imposed by the United States, cutlery firms in England and Germany went from exporting a large number of knives to seeing their employees migrate to the United States in the hopes of finding work. Those skilled workers, particularly from Sheffield, England, were instrumental in helping cutlery companies here get off the ground. Aside from the manpower, Sheffield's influence included the patterns of knives that were made in the United States, as well as the processes used to make them.

In addition to Sheffield, England and Solingen, Germany, knife-making processes and patterns in the United States were also influenced to a lesser degree by French, Spanish, Portuguese, and Italian tastes.

Over the years leading up to World War II, cutlery companies in states such as New York, Pennsylvania, and Connecticut rose and fell, as well as merged or split off to form new ventures. Cutlery companies were also wooed from one city to another, with other firms taking up the former digs via tax breaks and other incentives.

Backroom intrigues seemed to be a sign of the times in the early years. According to *Goin's Encyclopedia of Cutlery Markings*, the New York Knife Company was formed by striking workers from the Waterville Manufacturing Company in Waterbury, Connecticut In 1922, supervisors

Wooden shoes were worn in the grinding room to keep feet dry.

▲ Knife factory workers circa 1900.

employed at Schatt & Morgan started their own company, Queen City Cutlery Company, before buying out their former employers in 1928.

While there are certainly stories to be told for each of the cutlery companies that existed in towns and small cities, the primary focus here is on the overall Golden Age of cutlery.

Older is Not Always Better

Before we get started with the past, a stereotype exists in some collecting circles today that older knives are better than the knives made today. Anyone who has collected traditional pocketknives for even a short amount of time has, at some point, probably heard the phrase "They don't make 'em like they used

▲ While there were numerous variations of jack knives to choose from during the Golden Age of cutlery in the United States, Eureka jacks were among the more aesthetically pleasing.

to," or "There's nothing better than good old carbon steel."

Cutlery firms today certainly don't make knives like they did here in the United States from 1900 until World War II, but in most cases they make them better today due to advanced manufacturing processes, such as cutting out blades with lasers, better heat treatment of steels, new types of CPM tool steels, and modern stainless tool steels, such as 154CM.

But with that said, there's no doubt that traditional pocketknife companies, such as Case, Holley, Empire, Southington, Napanoch, New York Knife Company, Schatt & Morgan, Beaver Falls, Ulster, Union, Miller Brothers, Challenge Cutlery Company, Walden Knife Company, Waterville, etc., made traditional folding knives that lived up to most anyone's definition, then or now, of quality.

Fit and Finish: Hallmarks of Golden Age

Knives from the Golden Age are in demand by today's collectors because the companies attained a high level of workmanship using tools and processes that are crude by today's standards. (It was not a Golden Age for a grinder who was hunched over a grinding wheel day after day while choking down dust and grime.) They also continue to serve as inspirations to a new generation of custom knife makers who focus on the traditional patterns.

While the definition of quality is in the eye of each beholder, overall fit and finish is where most of the early cutlery companies in the United States excelled, and this was mainly due to those cutlers from Sheffield and Solingen.

The final fit and finish was often the task of the master cutler at the end of the knife-making assembly

Forging
hammers and
burly operators
in 1909.

▲ Knife duties in the early days were divided up among various workers, each of whom specialized in certain processes.

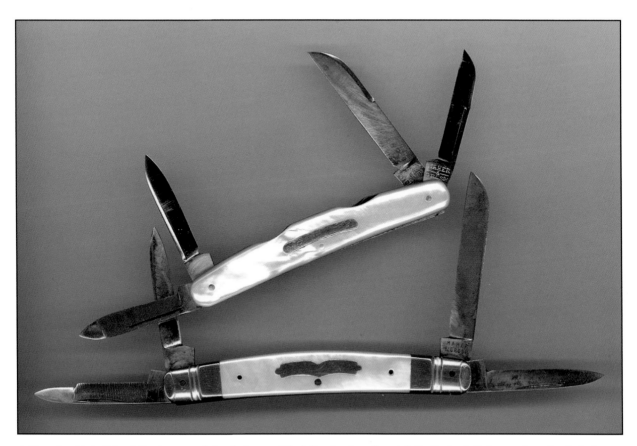

▲ These four-blade Maher & Grosh congress knives feature most the hallmarks of a well-made knife. The top knife has eased openings for better access to the nail pulls and even a long pull on the file blade. The congress on the bottom features elaborate bolsters and an unusual shield that follows the contours of the frame.

process. Prior to reaching the master cutler's stiddy, components, such as ground blades, were made by less skilled workers.

While wood, including cocobolo, ebony, and rosewood, and celluloid were used for the scales of working man's knives, such as jack knives, higher-end materials included mother-of-pearl (MOP), stag, water buffalo horn, elephant ivory, and jigged bone. Jigged bone, which was a less expensive alternative to stag and mother-of-pearl, became popular enough that two companies, Winterbottom Cutlery Works and Rogers Manufacturing Company, specialized in making scales out of cattle shin bones for the cutlery industry.

Physical attributes for a well-made knife include: mirror polished blades, match strike nail pulls, fluted bolsters, figured or embellished bolsters (fruit knives raised the bar on figured bolsters while the company name or logo on a barlow bolster served as advertising), swedges, company names stamped on each tang of a knife blade, and tipped, stepped, pinched, and grooved bolsters.

Excluding exhibition knives, knives of this era, both fixed blades and pocketknives, were tools made to be used, whether by businessmen who put penknives in their vest pockets, ladies that carried them in small clasp pouches, or multipurpose sportsmen's knives.

Of course, not all knives made during the Golden Age exhibited the best qualities. As the country's population grew, there was less of a demand for

▲ Union Cutlery Company first used the KA-BAR brand in the early 1920s. The KA-BAR dog's head shields adorn these three large folders.

higher-end knives and more market demand for less expensive knives, such as 10-cent or 15-cent barlow knives. The John Russell Company is known today for its barlow knives, but it made other high-quality knives, as well.

While smaller, more ornate knives, such as four-blade senators or lobster patterns, commanded the highest prices during the Golden Age, the reverse is true in collecting circles today. Large jack knives command such high prices today because the majority of them were used daily to perform a variety of cutting tasks. As a result, there are not many of them without worn-down blades or cracked handles. A lock back dirk by Holley that originally sold for $7.50 net per dozen could easily fetch more than $1,500 in prime condition.

The Demise of US Cutlery Companies

Pete Cohan, formerly the curator of the National Knife Museum, said it's misguided to attribute the fall of some of those early, high-quality cutlery companies to just the Depression or mechanization. The perfect storm began brewing in the late 1800s when the Sheffield companies started losing cutlers to American firms while they weren't being replaced in England.

"By 1900, the guild system in England had been squelched by Parliament, and that was the beginning of the end," Cohan said. "When that happened, there wasn't a sufficient number of people going into the apprentice system for training, and training could take ten to twelve years. A whole series of events that were associated with the lack of development of highly skilled cutlers began to take place."

The Tariff Acts of 1890, 1897, and 1901 dried up the export market in England, which forced Sheffield and Solingen cutlery employees to seek employment in the United States.

"As the cutlery companies here began to evolve, that reduced the demand for knives from England. They were losing their major export base," Cohan said. "These highly skilled people were the ones who

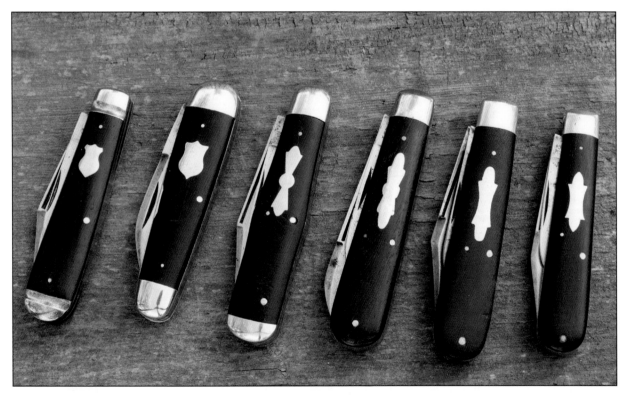

▲ Along with numerous patterns to choose from, knife buyers back in the day had their choice from hundreds of different shields.

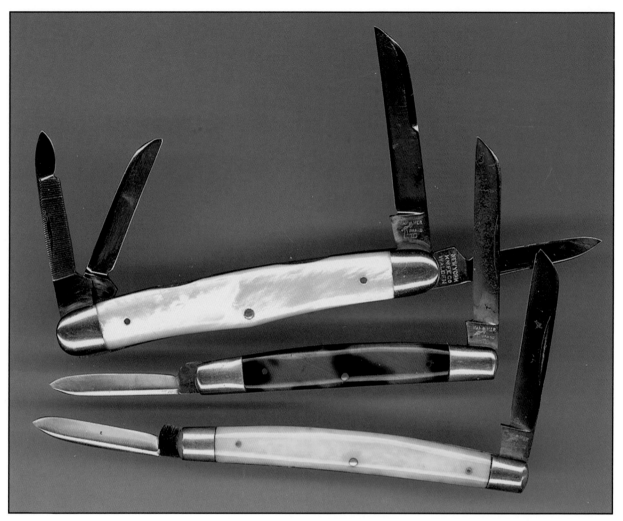

▲ In terms of fit and finish, the New York Knife Company was among the best before it went bankrupt in 1931. The top congress knife features mother-of-pearl scales, the middle tortoise with gold leaf backing, and the third elephant ivory.

did the final things that made these knives superlative. There were a lot of other factors, but certainly the loss of these highly skilled cutlers was the beginning of the end for a lot of these companies."

Most of the early cutlery companies mentioned previously had their brilliant arcs across the sky before eventually flaming out and closing their doors at various times after the turn of the century.

Demand for Quality Ebbs

Cohan said another factor was that high-quality knives became less important to the buying public in the United States, which was certainly driven home during the Depression.

"While there were many people who appreciated a fine quality knife, there were increasing generations of people who didn't have the same view on quality knives," he said. "They would actually be defined as being unable to differentiate strongly between an average or above average knife and a good, very fine piece. As this country began to grow, they weren't looking for—except for a limited, elite group, high-quality knives. They were looking for something they could buy at a very low cost that did the job.

"It was really a multilevel series of events and not the fact that someone walked in with a bunch of machines and told everybody else to take a walk."

▲ A vast array of knife patterns were made during the Golden Age of cutlery, including this brace of Rooster Nutters that were used for speying.

Remington Rides In

As the old-school cutlers died off, helped along by World War I in some cases, cutlery companies turned to mechanization to build their knives. Starting around 1919, Remington was able to draw upon a pool of employees, which included gunsmiths and tool and die employees, to build its own machines to make folding pocketknives in its Bridgeport, Connecticut plant. As a manufacturer of guns, typewriters, and other items, Remington had a company culture in regard to understanding the tolerances that were needed for quality knife manufacturing.

"As far as a highly mechanized cutlery company goes, Remington was the king of kings," Cohan said. "Clearly, they had an attention to detail and to tolerances that were a company mindset that was consistent with the type of businesses that they were in. You can't make a good gun if it has poor tolerances."

Not only could Remington out-produce the companies that were still hanging on with what was left of the highly skilled cutlers, but it also started competing against regional cutlery companies that weren't used to seeing competition in their backyards. For many of the regional companies, the competition was too keen.

▲ Daddy barlows with fish scalers by (left to right) Schrade, J. Russell, and Remington.

"The Depression was the downfall for a lot of these companies. Some were felled before then, but once Remington started producing a phenomenal number of knives a month and started selling them all over the US, these other companies couldn't keep up in markets that they once exclusively owned," Cohan said.

According to *Levine's Guide to Knives and their Values*, Remington had 907 patterns in its catalog by 1925, and in 1931 it announced that pocketknife production had exceeded 10,000 knives a day. While once "king of kings," Remington itself fell upon hard times later in the Depression before DuPont bought the company in 1933.

Mechanization Takes Over

With the onset of industrialization, blades were blanked with large presses. Instead of finishing those blades by hand, knife companies started putting batches of blades into large tumblers. While the end result was still a knife that cut, the knife blanks became smoother and rounded.

Knives that once featured slim profiles in pockets became bulkier with the new mechanized processes, and gaps between liners and springs became accept-able to the knife-buying public. After World War II, nations and companies moved on to other priorities.

"When we talk about American companies, there were so many that had their heyday," Cohan said. "Northfield, Schatt & Morgan, Cattaraugus, Beaver Falls, New York Knife Company, Ulster, Waterville, Empire, Southington, Walton, Excelsior, Humason & Beckley, Holley, American Knife Company. I could go on and on, but every one of these companies made an extremely high-quality knife. As they matured, fewer and fewer of their people were cutlers and more were machine operators as they slowly but surely converted from a largely hand operation to a largely machined operation.

"But every one of those companies had tremendously fine knives at some point during their histories and some of them throughout their lifespan. Some of them weren't around very long, but they produced an extremely high-end knife with fit and finish, style, and the right proportions. It's not surprising since a vast majority of these companies were started and run by cutlers mostly from England but certainly some from Germany, as well."

VII: When Cutlery was King: Knife Making in Sheffield

by Michael Critchlow

While there were many companies and countries that excelled in the manufacturing of cutlery, the city of Sheffield, England, was the crown jewel early on.

Sheffield became known worldwide as a Mecca for metallurgy and steel making and set the standard for the techniques and materials that were used for cutlery, as well as the knife patterns themselves. From an inauspicious start to an auspicious perch, Sheffield paved a bright path in the cutlery industry.

Rivers Key to Sheffield's Origin

In the Anglo-Saxon times, the area around Sheffield was known as Hallamshire, a name that is still in widespread use. Cutlery has been made in the Sheffield area for many hundreds of years.

Geoffrey Chaucer mentions the Miller of Trumpington, in "Reeve's Tale" from *The Canterbury Tales*, as having "a Sheffel thwitel baar in his hose." Chaucer was probably alluding to a whittle, an all-purpose knife commonly carried on the belt during the 14th century.

The city is located within the valleys of the River Don and its four tributaries, the Loxley, Porter, Rivelin, and Sheaf. The use of waterpower was a an important factor in the early industrialization of the area. Wherever possible weirs, or dams, were constructed and watermills and wheels built. Justice Fitzherbert, in his *Boke of Surveying* (1538), mentions scythe mills, cutler mills, and smith mills, as well as those used by the corn and wool merchants.

The Rivelin was once regarded as the home of the little mester, which was a self-employed freeman cutler. This area had at least twenty wheels, with some of those having more than one hull, or grinding shop. Each hull had a number of troughs, which was where the wet grinding wheels ran.

The Company of Cutlers in Hallamshire was established in 1624 by "an act for ye good order and government of ye makers of Knives, Sickles, Shears, Scissors, and other cutlery wares in Hallamshire in ye County of Yorke and the parts near adjoining."

By 1660, forty-nine sites on the Don or its tributaries had been dammed for grinding cutlery, forging iron, and growing corn. Starting around 1750, tilt mills, which were mills that had huge water-powered tilt hammers, and forges started to be built at certain sites. These giant hammers were used to work the iron and steel into more manageable and smaller pieces.

Steels Take Shape, Transportation Improves

On the raw materials front, forests surrounding the city were used to supply charcoal for smelting. Also, lower-quality ironstone deposits were found locally, as was coal. Much of the surrounding area to the west was overlaid with gritstone—a hard, coarse-grained, siliceous sandstone—that was quarried from ancient times for millstones and building materials. The abundance of these materials gave the town an early advantage over the other provincial cutlery centers and over the long haul, London.

Starting in about 1650, blister steel was produced in Sheffield. This skillful making process, which involved heating wrought iron together with charcoal in an airtight pot and carefully letting it cool over a period of about two weeks, produced a crude steel covered with blisters, giving it its name. Once they were forged and welded, these bars were made into shear steel, which was excellent for making knife blades.

One major problem for Sheffield in the early days was its transportation routes. Because it was situated in the heart of England, it was fairly inaccessible with all the routes to and fro being hilly and difficult to traverse. Over time, the River Don was made navigable for boats up to twenty tons, first from Doncaster to Tinsley, to Rotherham by 1740, then finally to near Sheffield by 1751. Then the roads were turn piked around 1756. The Don provided a quicker and cheaper link to London, and through it to overseas markets. It also made it easier to import raw materials, such as the high-grade iron ore from Sweden.

▲ This Elreb barlow features a shear steel blade, as well as integral iron bolsters and liners. It predates 1815 and was possibly made circa 1790. The knife was made by George Berley and Elreb is Berley spelled backwards minus the "y."

Coal, and more importantly coke, from the south Yorkshire coalfields was also brought up the river. The plentiful supply of quality fuel for the smithy fires was essential if the industry twenty to expand. Road and rail links continued to improve throughout the 19th century.

Sheffield and its surrounding area were by this time starting to make a name as a major center of cutlery manufacturing while emerging as a rival to London and York. The company, or guild, was formed to govern the industry, admit freemen, control apprenticeships, issue trademarks, and control the quality of the wares being made.

How They Were Made

The manufacture of cutlery started to increase toward the end of the 17th century, although it was still very much a cottage industry. Back then, most of the craftsmen, many of whom were little mesters, were largely making items for common consumption. Their workshops were relatively simple, small smithies that included a coal-fired hearth, bellows, stithy (more commonly known as an anvil or stiddy) mounted in a stock, an oak tree stump set deep into the ground, troughs, vices, hammers, and other tools and materials.

At the stithy, bar stock of blister or shear steel was heated and forged into blades. After forging, the blades were reheated and cooled in oil and water to prevent them from twisting. The cutler would then rent space at a wheel, perhaps a few hours a week, when he would grind his blades.

He would then glaze the blades using wooden wheels dressed with grinding compounds and polish them with a beeswax and suet leather covered wheel before finally polishing them with a rag dolly. At this

▲ This rare early George Brown knife was made circa 1790 and features hinged rear insert covers.

▲ A Levick penknife, 2⅞" closed, with tortoise shell and mother-of-pearl scales. This knife dates to around 1790 and features elaborate bolsters.

time, most of the freeman cutlers were part-timers, with many having small holdings and other part-time jobs. Knives tended to be single bladed and have integral iron liners and bolsters, which meant they were made from one piece. The best Sheffield steel would be reserved for the blade.

Crucible Steel

Benjamin Huntsman, a clockmaker from Doncaster, moved to Sheffield in 1740. Over the years, he had been trying to refine and improve steel for his clock springs, and Huntsman developed a method to make purified uniform steel.

The process involved using clay pots, or crucibles, which when white-hot were filled with pieces of blister steel and flux. When molten, the impurities were skimmed off and the steel was then poured into cast-iron molds. Once they cooled, the molds were broken open and the crucible steel, which was sometimes called cast steel, was removed. This whole process required a skilled workforce.

Crucible steel was more expensive, costing about a third more than shear steel. It was also more homogeneous and reliable, as well as tough and durable, and it could hold a good cutting edge.

Steam Power Takes Over, Trade Becomes Specialized

The first steam-powered grinding wheel was built in 1786. Over the next 60 to 70 years, steam power would dominate. By 1865, there were 32 water wheels versus 132 steam-powered ones. The steam-powered wheels allowed the cutlery firms to become more centralized. Gone were the days when cutlers, blade makers, drillers, hafters, cutters, etc. worked in their homes or nearby sheds and outbuildings.

Starting in 1820 and lasting until about 1850, there was an almost insatiable demand for knives, edged tools, and steel from North America. This demand sparked an enormous rise in the town's population at this time.

By the mid-19th century, all the various knife making trades were specialized, the craftsmen having served their apprenticeships and learned their specific trades, such as blade makers (grinders), hafters, etc.

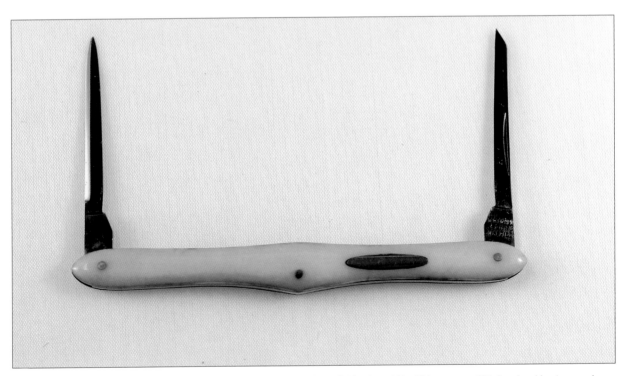

▲ It took a steady hand to grind the small blades of this Bright & Son tuxedo penknife, circa 1880, which measures 3⅜" closed and has ivory scales.

▲ This sportsman's knife by William Morton & Sons has checked ebony scales and was made around 1880 or 1890.

▲ This exhibition and display knife by John Petty & Sons from around 1900 features ivory scales inlaid with gold, silver, and copper, as well as file work on the backsprings and parts of the blades.

The forgers, grinders, and cutlers usually specialized in making certain types of knives. The proficiency and skill of these men were high. Apprentices were taken on at a young age, from ten to fourteen years old, and they served seven years working under their masters. Often sons followed their fathers and grandfathers in learning the same trade.

The making of a pocketknife would first involve a skilled forger who would, in his work room, backyard, or shed equipped with raw materials, use a simple coke-fired hearth, hand bellows, hammer, and bucket of water to forge the blades with dexterity and speed. The large hammer was used to work the tip. After reheating, and more work, the blade was cut off, reheated, and the tang formed. The blade would have the tang stamps and nail pulls cut and be quenched, hardened, and tempered using a whale oil solution.

A Knife Life

Albert Craven, a well-known forger, started out as a thirteen-year-old apprentice blade forger at Joseph Rodgers in 1906. He worked for seventy-two years until retiring in 1978.

At his job, Craven would take the mood, which is a rough blank or bar, and use his agon, which is an inverted chisel that is fitted cutting edge upward into the socket hole of his anvil. From there, he would cut in the kicks with his first few strikes. After the blade was fashioned, it was cut from the mood with a strike of the hammer. Albert used to boast he could make two gross at fourteen to the dozen ("grinders count") for a total of 336 blades in one day!

A grinder would be responsible for providing equipment and grindstones. A pocket blade grinder would buy a cowk, which was the center of a table grinder's stone. He would also have to provide his seat, leather belting, axles, working materials, etc.

Grinders sat astride horsing, which was a thick oak saddle shod with an iron fore and aft. Behind the grinder, in the same cast iron trow, would generally be the glazers, which were wooden leather-covered

▲ An equal-end whittler by George Wostenholm & Sons that was made circa 1920.

wheels dressed with glue and emery. There might also be a lap, which is a glazer with a lead surface further back.

The knife grinders were highly skilled. Before starting the day's work, the grinders would race (true up any irregularities) on their wheels to ensure even running and then clean them.

Knife blades would be ground in various stages; first rough ground to take out hammer marks, then finer to shape and smooth, and finally glazed on wooden-leather grit and emery-covered wheels. A visitor to Victorian Sheffield commented on a grinding hull, "The whole place is tinged with a peculiar brownish yellow hue," which was obviously settled dust and muck.

Grinders worked in horrendous conditions, often breathing fine dust from the stone and metal, while being cold, wet, and covered in muck. These conditions often ended with the grinders getting silicosis. The stones could burst, and they could also get caught up on the long drive belts. Many of these skilled craftsmen died before they reached middle age.

The blades and other knife parts, such as back springs, nickel silver linings, bolsters, and handle coverings, were made by other specialists prior to arriving on the cutler's bench.

Specialized Duties

As with many of the other trades, cutlers would specialize in making certain types of knives, and they would make those knives all their working lives.

Two-ended men would make the better-finished penknives. Pocket hands would work on single-ended pocketknives, such as lambfoot, sheepfoot, and pruners. It was the cutler's job to make the knife from all of the various component parts that were provided to him. Everything had to be fitted together perfectly, which was a process that was complex and required much skill.

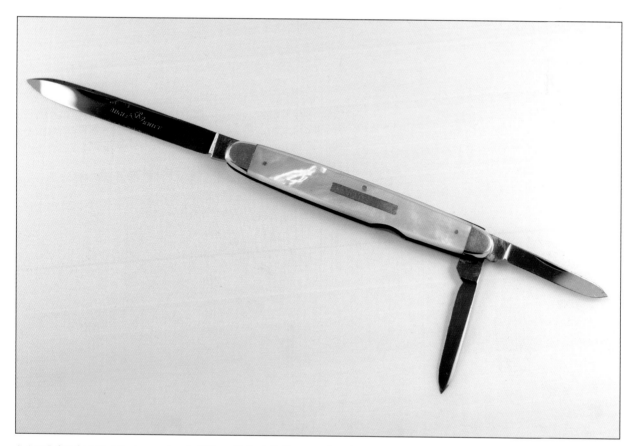

▲ A 4¼" closed Michael Hunter equal-end whittler with Bugle Knife stamped on the main blade and bugles stamped on the pen blades.

Best-finished knives, with milled linings, required much more work. The top cutlers knew many deft and clever ways to make these knives, which were the culmination of processes and methods learned over generations.

Employment conditions for all of the numerous trades involved in the knife-making process were varied and complex. A few larger firms preferred to employ workers under their own supervision, but they would often have to work alongside outworkers who were renting bench space. Most cutlery manufacturers, however, were content to rely on semi-independent or independent tradesmen, the little mesters.

Sheffield Comes of Age

Sheffield was a hive of activity with thousands of these skilled men and their apprentices renting space and power in the factories, public wheels, small workshops, and outbuildings. Together they made an infinite variety of wares. The workers would generally be paid on piecework, which meant they were only paid for the work done. While all of the prices were set, undercutting was common. Wages for the working men and women were generally poor.

The medium-sized cutlery business of John Watts, for example, manufactured and sold a huge selection of pen and pocketknives, as well as razors and other sundry items, including clog clasps and skating blades. Watts' particular specialty was multibladed, all-metal knives, such as champagne, electrician's, motoring, fishing, and sportsman's knives.

Every pattern was costed down to the smallest detail, including the linings, grinding, saw, buffing, plating, screws, and warehousing, but by far the largest cost was the cutler. The work was given either to their own workers, or the little mesters tradesmen who would probably be renting space and power in their Lambert Street works, or to outworkers who

▲ A four-inch sportsman's knife by Thomas Turner & Co.

specialized in making that particular sort of knife or knife part. Watts did supply materials for some jobs. Watts also bought best-finished knives from makers such as John Crossland, Joseph Haywood & Co., Ward & Morton, and Singleton & Priestman, although some of its wares were stamped with the Watts marks.

George Jackson of Bath Street was a particular favorite for supplying Watts-marked multibladed sportsmen's knives, which were superb, and large folding hunters. Watts bought large amounts of blade making bar from Flockton-Tompkin and B. Huntsman. Bowlers, which was a factor, supplied many parts and William Hutton the forks. The estimated profit margin on most the knives was 30 to 50 percent.

At this time, most of the knives that were made were town patterns, which were standard patterns made by all the manufacturers with all parts interchangeable between knives. Bowlers had more than five thousand sets of tools and dies of all the sizes with every one known by specific names. The cutler would bring in his pattern where it would be fitted into a blanking tool. With the blanking tool, the blades, liners springs, bolsters, and other parts would be found to fit.

The Decline

Cutlery manufacturing in both the United States and Germany increased rapidly during the second half of the 19th century. Most of these companies featured good designs that were mass-produced in modern factories.

Free of the archaic working practices prevailing in Sheffield and, in the case of the United States, protected by tariffs, these companies were better managed and equipped.

Faced with increased competition, a crumbling apprentice system, and protective tariffs abroad, many of the Sheffield cutlery workers migrated to the United States, where they were instrumental in helping forge the successes of early American cutlery companies.

▲ This Joseph Rodgers & Sons pruner (4¼" closed) with stag was made in the 1920s.

▲ While Sheffield's cutlery industry waned, companies such as George Wostenholm still made quality knives, including this utility knife from the 1930s.

Collecting Sheffield Knives

While Sheffield knives have been around for hundreds of years, there are some collecting tips for both beginners and experts including:

- Build a library of books and catalogs. *Tweedale's Directory* and *Levine's Guide to Knives and their Values, Fourth Edition"* are both good starting points.
- Multibladed knives should be checked to see if the makers' marks on all blade tangs are from the same maker.
- There was a mandatory requirement for the word England to be marked on English knives for export to the United States from 1891 onwards. It is often assumed that if the tang

mark doesn't include the word England, then the knife predates 1891. This might prove to be the case, but it is not always so.

- Many of the larger Sheffield cutlery firms made more than three thousand different pen and pocketknife patterns, and most of these patterns were standard throughout. It's quite possible to find knives made by different makers that look almost identical.
- Prior to about 1814, Sheffield manufacturers would mark their products with their touch-mark and maybe a simple word, pictorial mark, or both. For example, there was the Joseph Rodgers star and cross. Guild and legal rules were then altered allowing makers or factories to mark their finished cutlery with

more detail, including full name, address, or pictorial mark. Also at around this time, more complex stamping dies became affordable.

- Tradespeople supplying goods or services to members of the Royal Household could qualify for a Royal Warrant of Appointment. Royal Warrants lasted five years and then came up for review. A number of cutlery firms were granted these warrants over the years, and their wares were marked accordingly. It's quite a gray area, so it's perhaps best not to assume anything at face value.
- Caution is required when trying to estimate age, because Sheffield cutlers rarely threw anything away, which means residual stocks of knife parts, even marks, could be used decades after they were originally made.
- Best-finished knives were sometimes left in their component, or skeleton, form before being sent later to silversmiths and jewelers for decoration. These knives were made with linings that were ground slightly lower than the backspring and had a small notch at either end. Small hollow brass pins or rivets were made using wire or brass sheet or a brass sheet and a unique tool called a wortle. The skeleton knife was assembled using hollow brass pins. Then thin metal covers of silver or even gold were formed in special dies and applied using tabs at either end. These knives often have shackles, or bails.
- Drop-stamped blades were used in pocket knife manufacture from about 1890 onwards.
- Stainless steel blades became more available around 1920 and stainless backsprings from about 1930 on.
- Knives made after World War II are generally poorer quality, often having jigged bone or synthetic handle scales.

▲ A sportsman's all-metal knife by Thomas Turner & Company.

Abb. 22. Oelmühle oberhalb Hasenmühle. Nach einer farbigen Zeichnung von Artur Uellendall.

▲ The Wupper River and other streams in and around Solingen provided energy for waterwheels that in turn powered the cutting, grinding, and polishing of knife blades.

VIII: The Solingen Cutlery Trade

By Neal Punchard

Solingen was not the first city in the Germanic empire to produce cutlery, but it certainly became the most important. Cologne, Augsburg, and Nuremberg all predate Solingen in the production of cutlery, but Solingen has some deep roots, as well.

Dating back to the 15th century, Solingen produced many forms of blades from swords to pocketknives. While other towns were known for more elaborate or finely trimmed cutlery, Solingen's start was a bit more modest. Solingen's early pocketknives and tableware blades were solid and well-made but lacked the flash of silver or other fine details in the early years.

In the past, one common requirement for most major cutleries, or any major industry for that matter, was a source of power. Before the advent of electricity, waterpower from a river would power the wheels, which would in turn power the machines to cut, grind, and polish all parts of the knives. The Wupper River and several smaller streams ran through Solingen to provide that energy. With a good power source and the availability of local iron, Solingen's blade making industry continued to grow and prosper.

At the start of the 19th century, Napoleon Bonaparte's war throughout Europe resulted in years of blockades that prevented the export of Solingen cutlery. By the time the barrier was lifted a little more than a decade later, Solingen had fallen behind other major cutlery centers, namely Sheffield, England, in the export of its wares.

Solingen vs. Sheffield

Although Sheffield did indeed get a jump on Solingen in the way of export, especially to the new market in the United States in the early 1800s, Solingen took up the challenge. Agents from England were quick to set up distributorships in the United States, but meanwhile Germany was developing better factories.

Right up to the beginning of the twentieth century, most of the cutlery work in Sheffield and throughout England was done by little mesters. This essentially meant that each step of the cutlery work, from beginning to end, was done not in one location but by many individuals in small, independent shops. Many cutlers in Germany operated in a similar way, but only until the early 1800s when most companies started to do all their work under one roof. Not only did this help with better organization, but it also increased production as a result. These factories became efficient by the mid-1800s, and they were also developing a new power source in the form of steam. Steam power was a constant and reliable source of energy unaffected by river droughts or winter freeze ups.

US Market

By the late 1800s, Sheffield's cutlery industry was fading while Solingen's was coming on stronger than ever. The United States Tariff Act through the McKinley Bill of 1890 put a hard squeeze on all goods imported into the United States. The tariff was simply a tax on goods, including cutlery, which was imposed to help promote the sale of American products. This tariff was no small consequence, as it applied at minimum a 50 percent tax on most items imported to the United States. While this cut deep into the profits of Solingen cutleries, they continued steadily to sell their wares since the American knife trade could not meet the demand. In 1894, the McKinley Tariff was replaced by the Wilson-Gorman Tariff, which lowered the import taxes significantly. Unfortunately, as tariffs were being lowered to the German knife firms, the American knife companies were growing in strength and size.

Soon after, World War I started. The demand for weapons greatly boosted the German cutlery trade. The import of German knives to the United States all but stopped during the war but restarted again briskly afterward. By the 1920s, a great number of the American knife companies were well-established, yet the wares of many Solingen knife firms were also available. Many hardware store and sporting goods catalogs offered knives from Germany. They were usually listed as German-made or even simply imported. Two Solingen companies did retain strong name recognition in the United States: J.A. Henckels and H. Boker.

Henckels Shines

J.A. Henckels was one of the most respected cutlery companies not only in Germany, but throughout the

▲ Jagdmesser, which translates roughly to hunting knife, were popular patterns in Austria and Germany and were made by various cutlery companies. Some featured shotgun shell extractors while others came equipped with corkscrews.

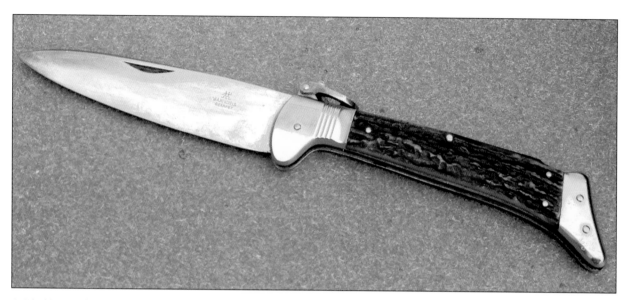

▲ A locking Henckels Jagdmesser that unlocks by pushing down on the ring when the blade is open. Despite appearances, the locking mechanism is quite stout.

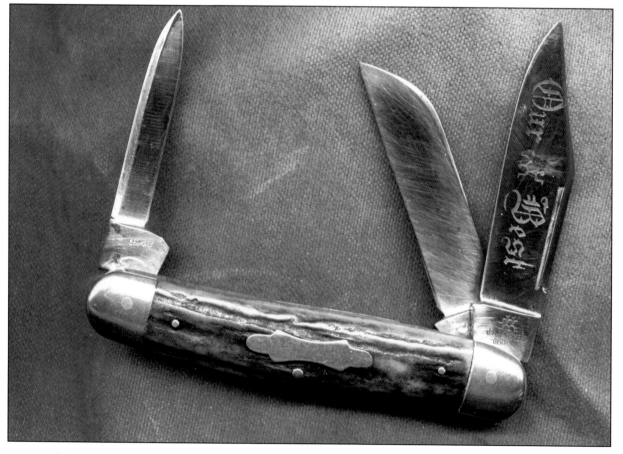

▲ J.A. Henckels' Our Best slogan purposely mimicked similar branding, such as Our Very Best which was used in the United States.

world. J.A. Henckels was founded in 1731 by Johann Peter Henckels, who introduced the famous twins logo, which looks like two stick people joined at the hip. By the late 1800s, the twins logo had become so well-recognized and admired that Henckels actually registered single, triple, and quadruple twins trademarks, which it never intended to use but rather designed and registered to keep others from using them.

It wasn't just the American customer who gave high praise to Henckels cutlery. At the first great World's Fair of 1851, which took place at the Crystal Palace in London, England, Henckels started winning the top awards. It continued to win the highest honors at subsequent world exhibitions in Paris in 1855, Chicago in 1893, and San Francisco in 1915.

In 1939, Henckels invented a new process of blade hardening called Friodur, which was a special type of ice hardening. This method was so successful that Henckels actually stamped its knives with Friodur, along with its twins logo, on a wide range of models. In the 1960s, Henckels stopped producing pocketknives to concentrate on its more lucrative kitchen line of cutlery. The company did however continue to sell folding pocketknives; these were contracted to other German manufacturers but carried the Henckels name.

Boker Blossoms

A second German cutlery powerhouse was, of course, Boker. Arriving on the scene much later than J.A. Henckels, Heiner. Böcker and Co. (note the original spelling) was founded in 1869 by Heinrich Bocker and Hermann Heuse. The name was later changed to H. Boker. This German-based company was originally started to supply knives to relatives who had set up shops in both Mexico City and New York. While Henckels had its famous twins logo, Boker had an equally famous tree logo, a replica of a giant chestnut tree that once stood over the original Boker shop.

Although the H. Boker brand was known throughout the world, its history was less clear and quite convoluted. Perhaps one of the most confusing aspects of Boker was that there were actually two separate Boker companies that worked hand in hand and were based out of Solingen, Germany, and New York City. The New York H. Boker company sold Boker-marked knives that were made both in Germany and America, confusing matters even more. Although the tree logo was used consistently on almost every knife, various Boker name stampings were produced during different time periods.

Starting in the early 1900s, H. Boker promoted and sold its knives in more hardware and sporting goods stores across the United States than any other German firm. The major hardware stores of the time that didn't have their own private lines of cutlery, such as Shapleigh's and Hibbard, Spencer & Bartlett, would often feature Boker knives as their main product lines.

World War II

When World War II started, all German goods were embargoed. However, since Boker had a manufacturing company in the United States, it was the only German-based knife company to continue to sell knives in the United States. In fact, Boker supplied knives to the US military during World War II. After the war, Boker's strong sales continued and the company was sold to the Wiss & Sons Company in the early 1960s. The new owner kept the Boker name and knife sales flourished.

A series of books would hardly cover the history of the Solingen cutlery trade, so this chapter is but a short sample. Germany, and Solingen specifically, produced more cutlery in the late 19th century to early 20th century than any other country.

Not only did they produce the most, they also produced some of the best knives during that time period. Aside from standard production knives and swords, Solingen also manufactured a great number of exhibition-grade cutlery that rivaled any others, past or present.

Currently, knives from Solingen, especially pre-World War II models, are often overlooked and undervalued by many collectors. The high quality blade steel and premium handle materials combined with the excellent fit and finish make Solingen cutlery a valued collectible for all enthusiasts from novice to expert.

Schleiferei

▲ Grinders working at the J.A. Henckels plant. Grinding wheels could be more than five feet tall, and in this instance, two grinders are working on the top and front of each wheel. PHOTO CREDIT: ZWILLING J.A. Henckels AG, Germany

◄ Henckels workers use a rack hammer to forge the steel for knife blades and other items.
PHOTO CREDIT: ZWILLING J.A. Henckels AG, Germany

Schaufenster-Dekoration im typischen Henckels-Stil

▲ A typical display window by Henckels. At the height of its production, Henckels' product line featured thousands of different items, including fencing equipment, swords, scissors, cigar cutters, trade-specific knives, and kitchen utensils.
PHOTO CREDIT: ZWILLING J.A. Henckels AG, Germany

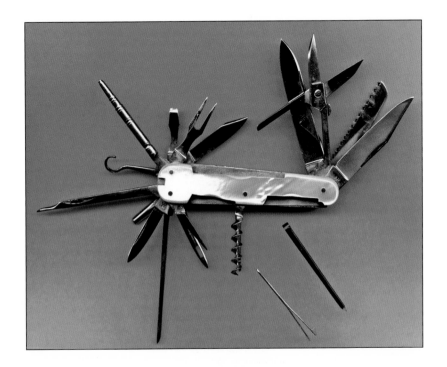

◄ This pearl-handled Henckels combination knife has twenty different implements, including tweezers and a tortoise shell toothpick inserted into the frame and scales.

▲ A top view of one side.

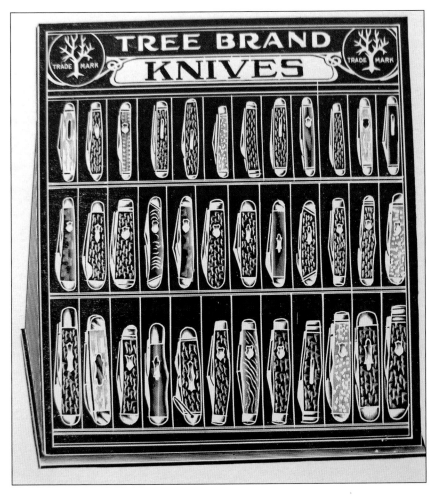

◀ Boker's tree logo was well-known both here and abroad.

▲ At more than four inches closed, this four-blade Boker congress was ready for just about any cutting task.

▲ This Boker canoe features a punch blade, as well as pinched and grooved bolsters.

Notable names of German companies

J.A. Henckels and H. Boker were just two of the hundreds of quality cutlery companies that originated in Solingen, Germany. The following is a short list of some of the more well-known Solingen cutleries, listed alphabetically by last name.

- Boentgen & Sabin, 1870 to 1983. Main trademark: Bonsa. Produced a wide array of knives and other cutlery under its brand, as well as contract knives for others.
- Joseph Feist, 1880 to 1968. Main trademark: the Greek letter Omega Ω. Produced all types of cutlery from pocketknives to razors and scissors.

- Gebruder Grafrath, 1869 to c. 1940s. Main trademark: a flying W. Produced all types of cutlery, as well as daggers and bayonets for the German army.
- Gottlieb Hammesfahr & Co., 1804 to 1994. Main trademark: a pyramid. Produced all types of cutlery and specialized in drop forging.
- Friedr. Herder, 1623 to 1994. Main trademarks: a spade and crossed keys. Produced all types of cutlery and was Solingen's oldest surviving cutlery company when it shut down in 1994.
- Heinrich Kaufmann & Sohne, 1856 to present. Main trademarks: flowers and Mercator. Produced

▲ A couple of Boentgen & Sabin, or Bonsa, stockman knives.

all types of cutlery and was self-described early on as a merchant to East India, China, and Japan.

- Robert Klaas, 1869 to c. 1980. Main trademark: two storks. Produced all types of cutlery but focused mainly on export trade to North America.
- Carl Linder, 1870 to present. Main trademark: a crown with a cross on top. Produced mostly pocket and hunting knives.
- Daniel Peres, 1792 to present. Main trademark: a wooden barrel. Produced mostly folding and fixed-blade knives for themselves and on contract for others.
- Puma, 1922 to present. Started by the Lauterjung family, which had been in the knife manufacturing business since 1769. Main trademark: the head of a puma. Produced folding and hunting knives and are best known for their White Hunter sheath knife.

- J. A. Schmidt & Sohne, 1829 to c. 1940s. Main trademark: Hubertus. Produced all types of cutlery and various tools. The name Hubertus was acquired by Kuno Ritter in 1950, who shortly thereafter renamed his company Hubertus.
- Wilh. Weltersbach, 1882 to 1994. Main trademark: Weidmannsheil, which translates to good hunting. Produced folding and fixed-blade knives, as well as lever lock switchblades for themselves and under contract for others.
- Anton Wingen Jr., 1888 to 1996. Main trademark: the head of Othello. Produced pocketknives and other cutlery for itself and on contract for others.

IX: Knife Pictorial and Values

The following section serves up various knives and their estimated values. There are several books that provide detailed knife-related values, but with the birth of eBay, knife prices can be fluid. One wealthy collector can have an impact on a certain pattern's prices if he or she is buying up everything in sight. Other high-end knives don't see the light of day on eBay but are instead purchased at knife shows or passed around among a group of dealers and buyers.

As mentioned previously, look at the third-highest bidder on the bidding history of a completed knife auction on eBay instead of the final price. The two highest bidders may have inflated the value during a bidding war.

Since specific knife values are snapshots in time at best, I've provided value ranges for each knife that follows. In some instances, the value ranges reflect the amount that the buyers paid. In others, knife experts and dealers weighed in with their estimates. Lastly, some of the value ranges came from eBay searches and knife prices on Web sites. In the end, decide what you are willing to pay for a given knife, and don't buy into a seller telling you what the book value is.

For patterns, I have tried to use the traditional names, although in some cases different companies had their own names for certain patterns. I have included more recent names that collectors currently use in quotation marks. Also, some companies referred to their jigged bone as stag jigged bone, when, in fact, it was cattle shin bone.

Jack knives

Pattern: Large cigar, equal-end jack (double shield)
Company: Hibbard, Spencer, Bartlett Hardware and Company, Our Very Best

Closed length: 4¼"
Handle material: Jigged bone
Value range:. . . . . $300–$350

Pattern: Jumbo jack
Company: Union Cutlery Company
Closed length: 4

Handle material: Stag
Value range:.........................$300–$350

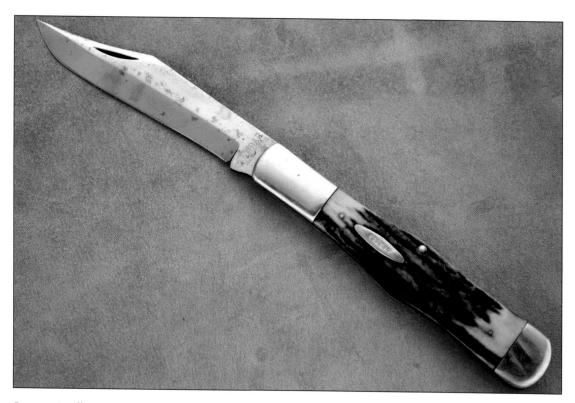

Pattern: Swell-center hunter, "cokebottle," "fiddle-back," "beavertail"
Company: KA-BAR

Closed length: 5¼"
Handle material: Stag
Value range:.....................$800–$850

Pattern: Slim swell-center hunter
Company: KA-BAR
Closed length: 5⅜"

Handle material: Jigged bone
Value range:. . . . .$800–$850

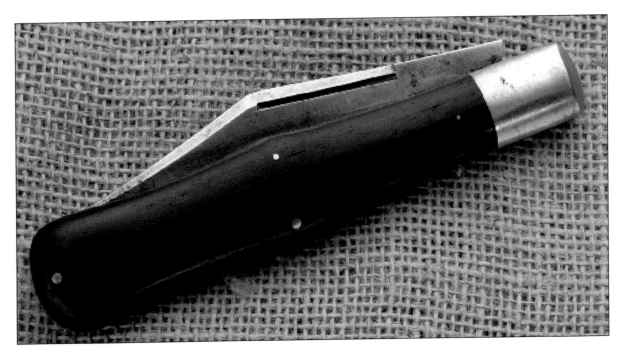

Pattern: Swell-center hunter, "cokebottle," "fiddleback,"
"beavertail"
Pattern number: 189
Company: New York Knife Company, Hammer Brand

Closed length: 5½"
Handle material: Ebony
Value range:. . . . .$400–$450

Pattern: Swell-center hunter, "cokebottle," "fiddleback," "beavertail"
Pattern number: 187
Company: New York Knife Company, Hammer Brand

Closed length: 5½"
Handle material: Stag jigged bone
Value range:...................... **$450–$550**

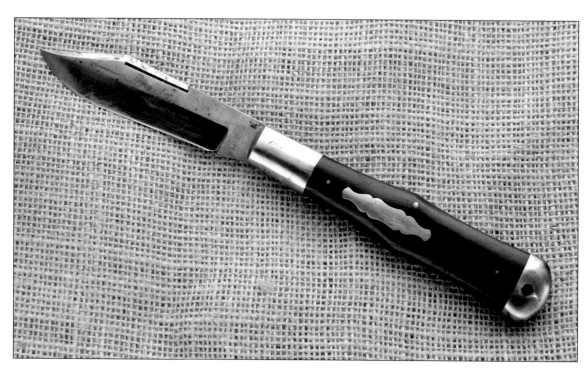

Pattern: Swell-center hunter, "cokebottle," "fiddle-back," "beavertail"
Company: Challenge Cutlery Company (Bridgeport, Connecticut), Daniel Boone etch

Closed length: 5⅜"
Handle material: Ebony
Value range:...................... **$400–$425**

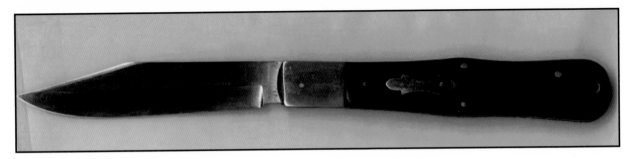

Pattern: Swell-center hunter, "cokebottle"
Company: J.A. Henckels
Closed length: 5¼"

Handle material: Ebony
Value range:. . . . .$150–$175

Pattern: Swell-center hunting knife with swing guard
Company: Ulster
Closed length: 5⅜"

Handle material: Ebony
Value range:. . . . .$400–$450

Pattern: Swing-guard hunter
Company: KA-BAR
Closed length: 5¼"

Handle material: Stag
Value range:. . . . .**$1,500–$1,600**

Pattern: Large trapper, "Bullet"
Pattern number: R1128
Company: Remington Arms Company

Closed length: 4½"
Handle material: Cocobolo
Value range:. . . . . **$1,500–$1,700**

Pattern: Large trapper, "Bullet"
Pattern number: R1123
Company: Remington Arms Company

Closed length: 4½"
Handle material: Jigged bone
Value range:........$1,800–$2,200

Pattern: Large trapper, dog's head shield
Company: Union Cutlery Company, KA-BAR
Closed length: 4½"

Handle material: Feather jigged bone
Value range:............... $1,200–$1,300

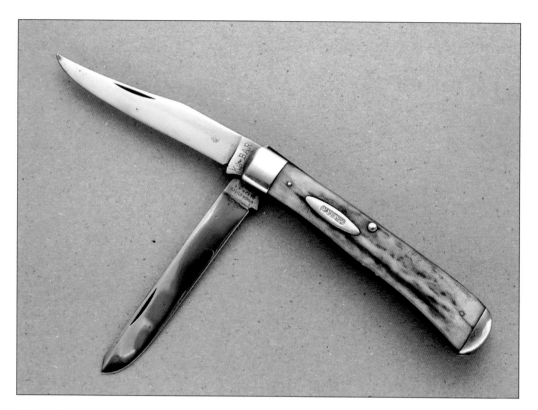

Pattern: Large trapper
Company: Union Cutlery Company, KA-BAR
Closed length: 4⅛"

Handle material: Stag
Value range:. . . . . **$150–$200**

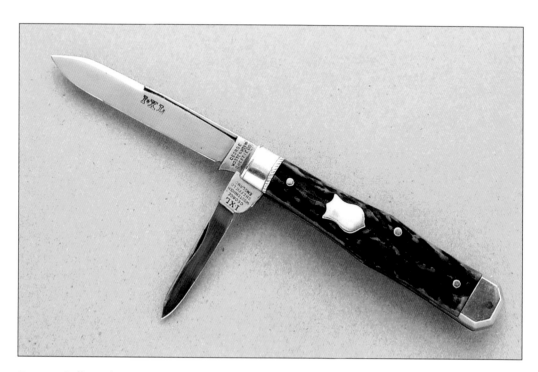

Pattern: Coffin jack
Company: George Wostenholm, IXL
Closed length: 3½"

Handle material: Stag
Value range:. . . . . **$400–$500**

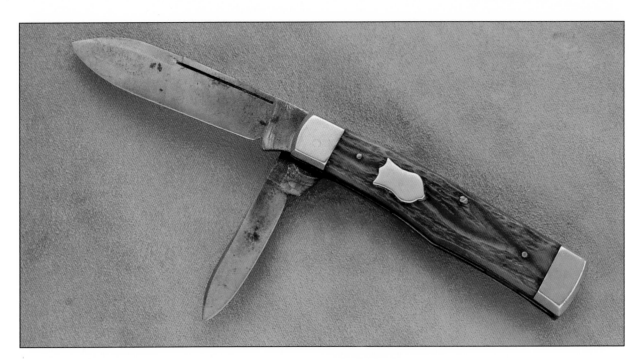

Pattern: Gunstock jack
Company: Schatt & Morgan
Closed length: 3½"

Handle material: Jigged bone
Value range:. . . . . **$125–$150**

Pattern: Sleeveboard jack
Company: Cattaraugus Cutlery Company
Closed length: 4½"

Handle material: Rogers Indian Trail jigged bone
Value range:. . . . . **$400–$450**

Pattern: Sleeveboard jumbo jack
Company: Camillus
Closed length: 3¾"

Handle material: Ebony
Value range:........................**$150–$175**

Pattern: English Jack
Company: Damascus Steel Products, DASCO
Closed length: 4½"

Handle material: Jigged bone
Value range:........................**$175–$200**

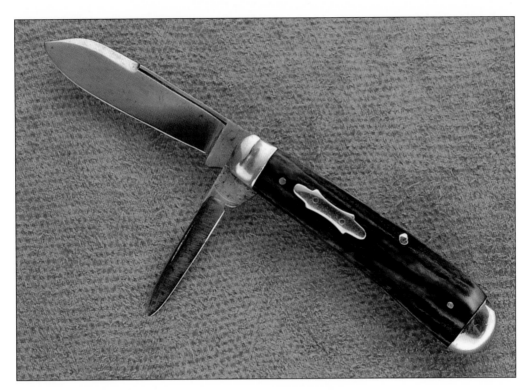

Pattern: Curved jack
Company: Early Keen Kutter, E.C. Simmons
Hardware

Closed length: 3½"
Handle material: Stag
Value range:.................\$300–\$350

Pattern: Eureka jack
Company: Marshall Wells Hardware Company
(made by New York Knife Company)

Closed length: 3¾"
Handle material: MOP
Value range:.................\$400–\$450

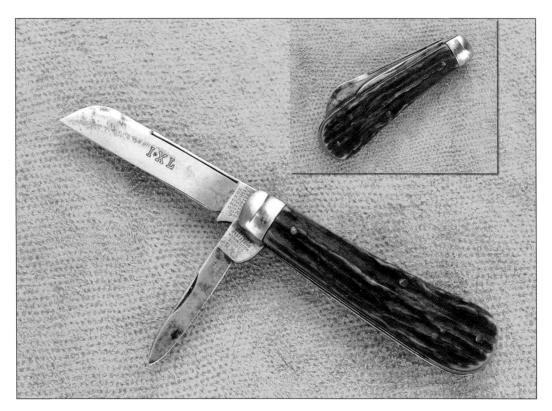

Pattern: Swayback jack
Company: George Wostenholm, IXL
Closed length: 3⅝"

Handle material: Stag
Value range:.....................$300–$350

Pattern: Jumbo jack
Company: Early Keen Kutter, E.C. Simmons
Hardware

Closed length: 4"
Handle material: Jigged bone
Value range:.....................$150–$175

Pattern: Candle-end jack
Company: Empire Knife Company
Closed length: 3 1/16"

Handle material: Ebony
Value range:. . . . . **$100–$125**

Pattern: Barlow jack
Company: KA-BAR
Closed length: 3 3/8"

Handle material: Smooth bone
Value range:. . . . .**$100–$125**

Pattern: Barlow
Company: George Wostenholm, IXL
Closed length: 3⅜"

Handle material: Ebony
Value range: . . . .**$150–$175**

Pattern: Barlow
Company: George Wostenholm, IXL
Closed length: 3⅜"

Handle material: Sawcut bone
Value range:. . . . .**$125–$140**

Pattern: Barlow
Company: Edward K. Tryon
Closed length: 3½"

Handle material: Sawcut bone
Value range:................. **$100–$125**

Pattern: Daddy barlow
Pattern number: R1240
Company: Remington Arms Company

Closed length: 5"
Handle material: Sawcut bone
Value range:................. **$400–$450**

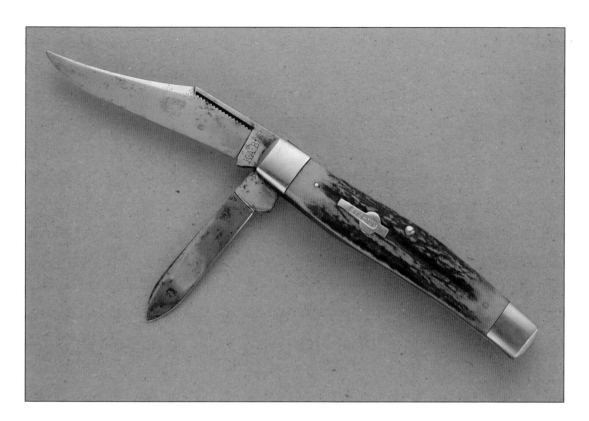

Pattern: Texas jack
Company: KA-BAR
Closed length: 4¼"

Handle material: Stag
Value range:....................**$400–$450**

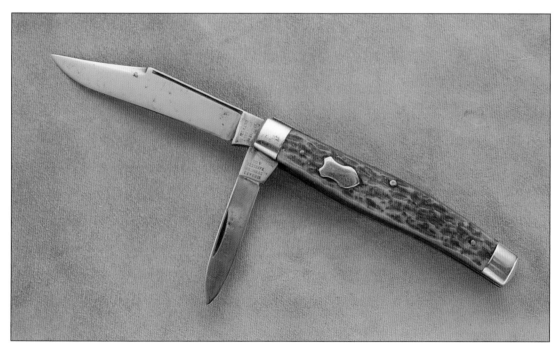

Pattern: Texas jack
Company: Hibbard, Spencer, Bartlett Hardware
and Company

Closed length: 3⅞"
Handle material: Jigged bone
Value range:.................**$150–$175**

Pattern: Folding hunter
Company: Case
Closed length: 5¼"

Handle material: Late Rogers Jigged bone
Value range:.....................**$550–$600**

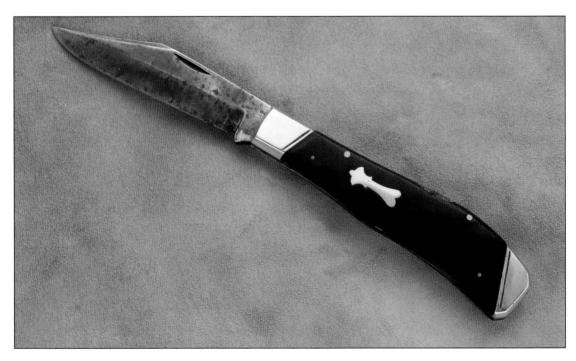

Pattern: Arkansas Hunter
Company: Empire Cutlery Company
Closed length: 4½"

Handle material: Ebony
Value range:.....................**$450–$500**

Pattern: Lockback
Pattern number: 1665
Company: New York Knife Company

Closed length: 4½"
Handle material: Stag jigged bone
Value range:................... $550–$650

TOP
Pattern: Swing-guard lockback
Company: J.A. Henckels
Closed length: 4¼"
Handle material: Stag
Value range:................. $500–600

BOTTOM
Pattern: English jack, lockback
Company: J.A. Henckels
Closed length: 4½"
Handle material: Stag
Value range:................. $550–$650

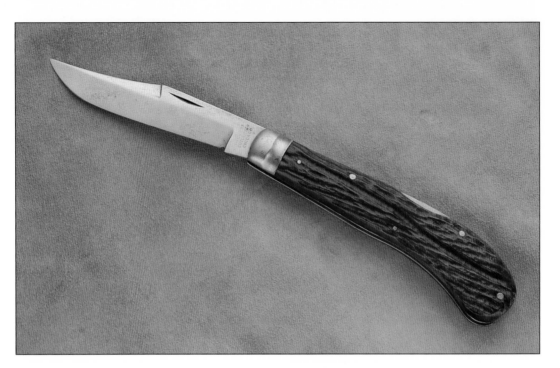

Pattern: Saddlehorn
Company: Wilbert Cutlery Company (made by Napanoch)

Closed length: 4⅝"
Handle material: Worm groove jigged bone
Value range: . . . . **$950–$1,000**

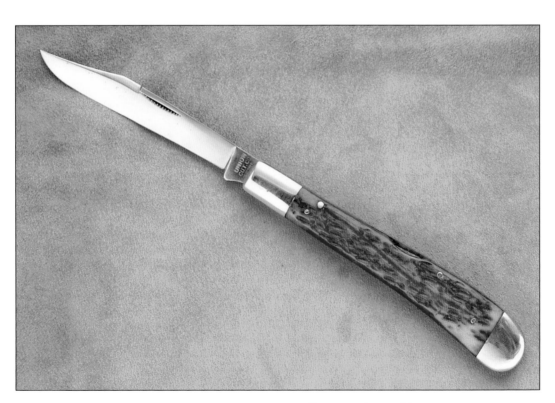

Pattern: Banana jack, lockback
Company: Union Cutlery Company
Closed length: 5¼"

Handle material: Jigged bone
Value range: . . . . **$1,000–$1,200**

Pattern: Banana jack, lockback
Company: Valley Forge Cutlery Co.
Closed length: 5¼"

Handle material: Jigged bone
Value range:....................$250–$300

Pattern: Banana jack, lockback
Company: Winchester Arms Company
Closed length: 5¼"

Handle material: Stag
Value range:.................$2,400–$2,500

Pattern: Banana jack, lockback
Pattern number: R1253
Company: Remington Arms Company

Closed length: 5⅜"
Handle material: Stag jigged bone
Value range:...................$1,500–$1,600

Pattern: Banana jack, lockback
Company: Napanoch
Closed length: 5¼"

Handle material: Jigged bone
Value range:........$1,450–$1,550

Pattern: Yukon, "King of the Woods" linerlock with factory bail
Company: Cattaraugus Cutlery Company
Closed length: 5¼"
Handle material: Rogers Indian Trail jigged bone
Value range:. . . . . **$1,200–$1,300**

Pattern: Serpentine jack
Company: Carrier Cutlery Company
Closed length: 3½"
Handle material: MOP
Value range:. **$350–400**

Pattern: Swell-center jack
Company: Keen Kutter
Closed length: 3¾"

Handle material: Brown jigged bone
Value range:. **$350–$450**

Pattern: Double-end jack, "moose"
Company: Camillus Cutlery Company (four-line stamp)

Closed length: 4¼"
Handle material: Brown jigged bone
Value range:. **$500–$600**

Pattern: Double-end premium jack, "moose"
Pattern number: 2399
Company: New York Knife Company

Closed length: 3¾"
Handle material: Stag jigged brown
Value range:. **$600-700**

Pattern: Swell-center or balloon jack
Company: Empire Knife Company
Closed length: 3½ "

Handle material: Ebony
Value range:. . . . .**$450–$550**

Pattern: Equal-end jack
Company: Clauss Cutlery Company
Closed length: 4¼"

Handle material: Jigged bone
Value range:.......................$500–$650

Pattern: Easy-opener jack
Company: Nagle Reblade Knife Company

Closed length: 3⅝"
Value range:.......................$600–$700

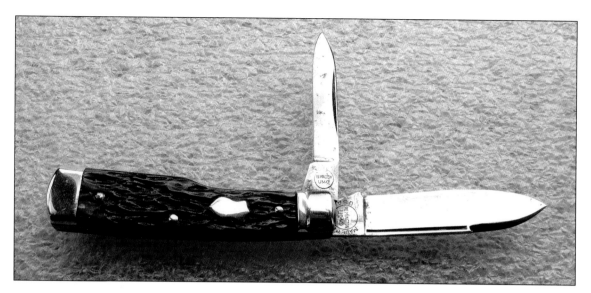

Pattern: Gunstock jack
Pattern number: R683
Company: Remington Arms Company

Closed length: 3"
Handle material: Jigged brown bone
Value range:. . . . .**$400–$500**

Pattern: Regular jack
Pattern number: R101 with salesman's numbers
Company: Remington Arms Company

Closed length: 3½"
Handle material: Rosewood
Value range:. . . . .**$300–$325**

Pattern: Regular jack
Company: Remington Arms Company
Closed length: 3½"

Handle material: Ebony
Value range:. . . . .$200–$250

Pattern: Regular jack (barehead)
Company: Napanoch
Closed length: 3¼"

Handle material: Ebony
Value range:. $250–300

Pattern: Regular jack
Company: Holley Manufacturing Company
Closed length: 3¾"

Handle material: Buffalo horn
Value range:. . . . .**$300–$350**

Pattern: Regular jack
Company: Keen Kutter, E.C. Simmons
Closed length: 3¾"

Handle material: Ebony
Value range:. . . . .**$150–$175**

Pattern: Swell-center stabber jack
Company: Connecticut Cutlery Co., Naugatuck, Connecticut.

Closed length: 3¾"
Handle material: Rosewood
Value range:. . . . . **$250–$300**

Pattern: Serpentine jack, dogleg
Company: Empire Knife Co.
Closed length: 3⅝"

Handle material: Rosewood
Value range:. . . . . **$150–$175**

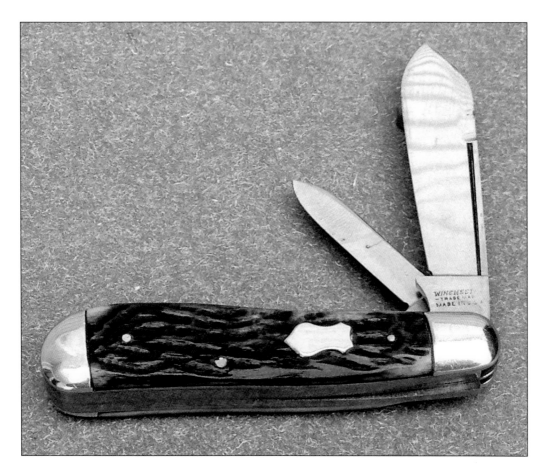

Pattern: Serpentine jack, dogleg
Company: Winchester Arms
Full length: 3½"

Handle material: Early Winchester jigged bone
Value range:...................$400–$600

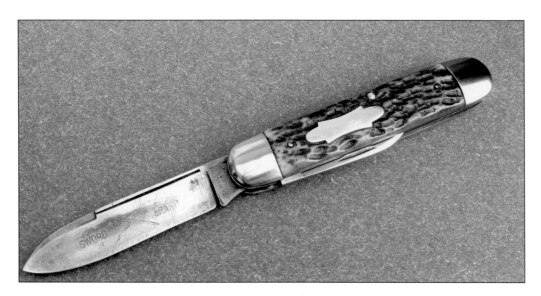

Pattern: Equal end, cigar jack
Company: Camillus (premium Sword brand)
Closed length: 4⅛"

Handle material: Jigged bone
Value range:.................. $150–$170

Pattern: English jack
Company: George Wostenholm, IXL
Closed length: 4¾"
Handle material: Stag
Value range:...............$500–$600

Pattern: English jack
Company: George Wostenholm, IXL
Closed length: 4⅛"

Handle material: Stag
Value range:....................$600–$650

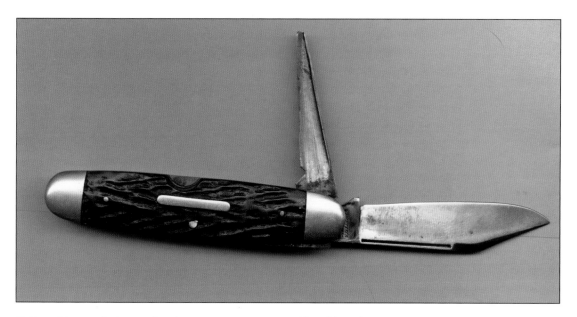

Pattern: Harness jack, equal end
Pattern number: 2927
Company: Winchester Arm

Closed length: 3⅜"
Handle material: early Winchester jigged bone
Value range:......................**$250–$300**

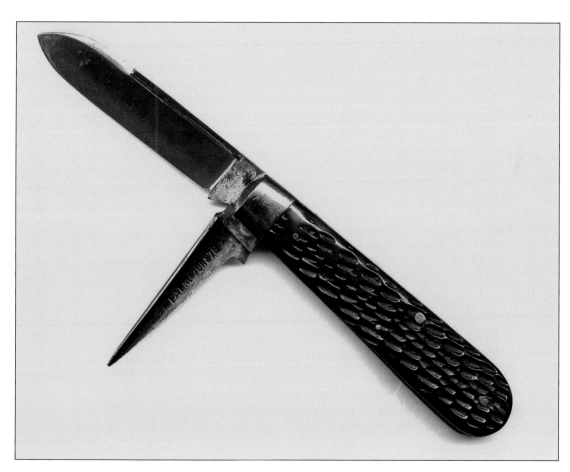

Pattern: Harness jack
Company: Eagle, Philadelphia (factory second by NYK Co.)

Closed length: 3½"
Handle material: Jigged bone
Value range:......................**$150–$170**

Pattern: Regular jack
Company: George Wostenholm, IXL
Closed length: 3½"

Handle material: Buffalo horn
Value range:. . . . .$135–$155

Pattern: Muskrat jack
Pattern number: R4593
Company: Remington Arms Company

Closed length: 3⅝"
Handle material: Jigged brown bone
Value range:. . . . .$150–$200

Pattern: Fish knife with hook disgorger cap, Texas toothpick
Pattern number: R1613
Company: Remington Arms Company

Closed length: 5"
Handle material: Jigged brown bone
Value range:. . . . . **$450–$500**

Pattern: Doctor's knife, jack with advertisement
Company: Utica Cutlery Co.

Closed length: 3¾"
Handle material: MOP
Value range:. . . . . **$650–$750**

Pattern: Sowbelly stockman
Company: John Pritzlaff Hardware Company
Closed length: 3¾"

Handle material: Jigged brown bone
Value range: . . . .$450–$550

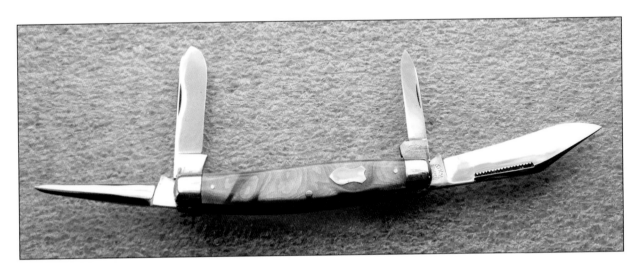

Pattern: Premium stockman with punch from factory collection
Pattern number: Salesman sample No. 441011/1018
Company: Utica

Closed length: 4"
Handle material: Celluloid
Value range: . . . .$750–$850

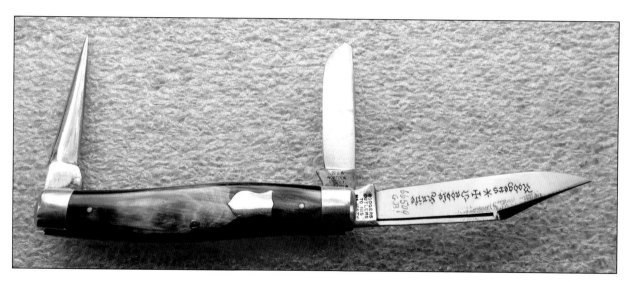

Pattern: Stockman
Pattern number: Salesman sample No. 86509 GB
Company: Joseph Rodgers & Company

Closed length: 4"
Handle material: Black buffalo horn
Value range:. . . . . **$900–$1,000**

Pattern: Junior Cattle Knife with punch
Pattern number: 6336
Company: New York Knife Co., Hammer Brand

Closed length: 3⅛"
Handle material: Brown jigged bone
Value range:. . . . . **$450–$500**

Pattern: Stockman
Company: Schrade Cutlery Company
Closed length: 3⅛"

Handle material: Abalone celluloid
Value range:. . . . .$175–$190

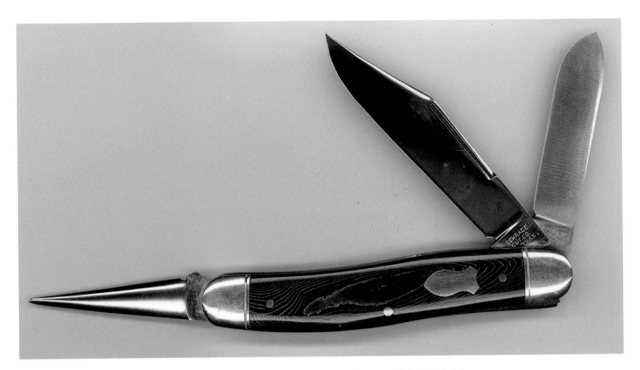

Pattern: Serpentine stockman (with punch)
Company: Schrade Cutlery Company
Closed length: 3½"

Handle material: Celluloid
Value range:. . . . .$200–$225

Whittlers

Pattern: Equal-end whittler, tipped bolsters
Company: Hibbard, Spencer, Bartlett Hardware and Company, Our Very Best
Closed length: 3½"
Handle material: Jigged bone
Value range:. . . . . $150–$175

Pattern: Jumbo sleeveboard whittler with punch
Company: Hibbard, Spencer, Bartlett & Co., OVB
Closed length: 3⅝"
Handle material: Ebony
Value range:. . . . . $250–$300

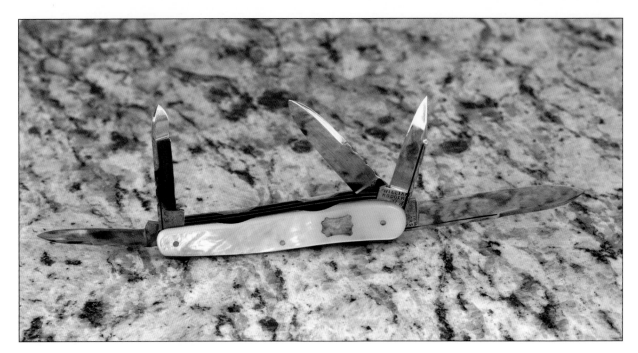

Pattern: Serpentine whittler, shadow
Company: William Rodgers
Closed length: 3¼"

Handle material: MOP
Value range:. $350–450

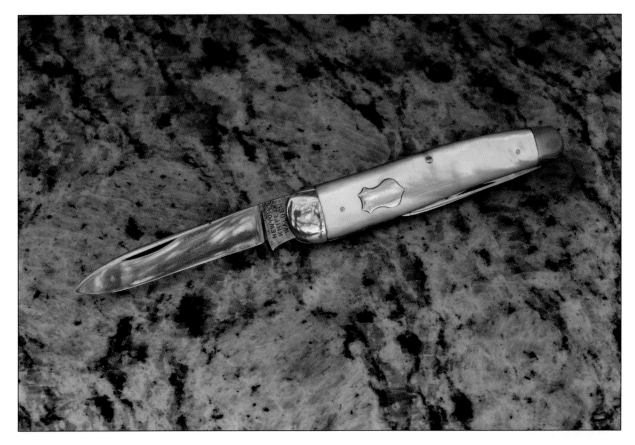

Pattern: Serpentine whittler
Company: New York Knife Company
Closed length: 3¼"

Handle material: MOP
Value range:. . . . .$250–$325

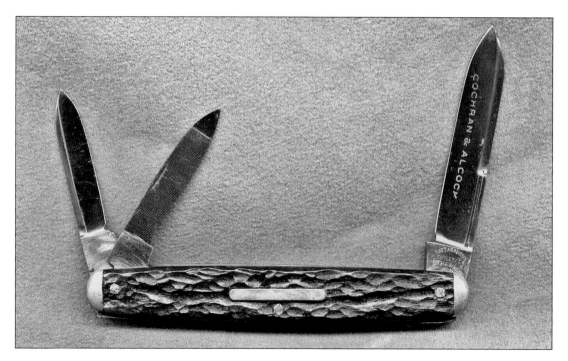

Pattern: Whittler
Pattern number: 33689
Company: Cattaraugus Cutlery Company

Closed length: 3½"
Handle material: Rogers Indian Trail jigged bone
Value range:. . . . .$250–$275

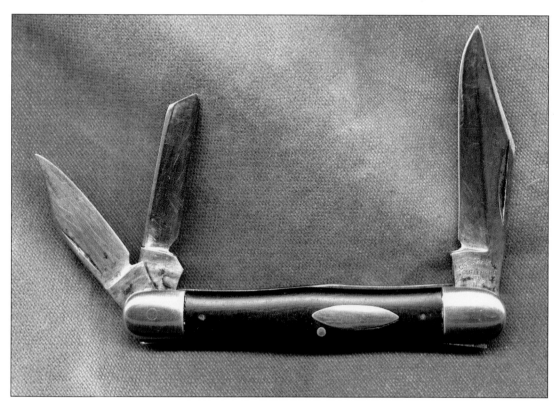

Pattern: Swell-center whittler
Company: Cattaraugus Cutlery Company
Closed length: 3½"

Handle material: Ebony
Value range:. . . . . $100–$150

Pattern: Norfolk whittler
Company: Joseph Rodgers & Sons
Closed length: 3⅞"

Handle material: Ivory
Value range:. . . . .**$700–$900**

Congress Knives

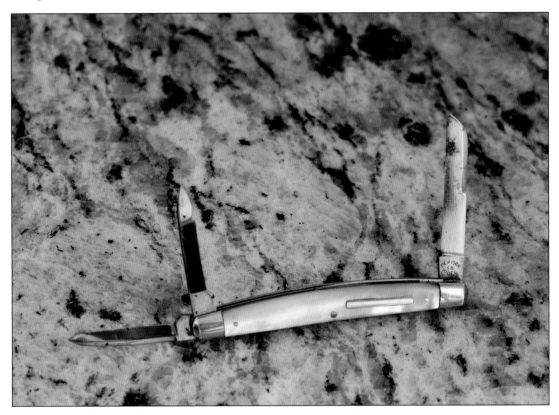

Pattern: Congress, four blades
Pattern number: 446
Company: New York Knife Company

Closed length: 2¾"
Handle material: MOP
Value range:. . . . .**$300–$350**

Pattern: Swell-center congress
Company: Brookes & Crookes
Closed length: 2⅛"

Handle material: MOP
Value range:. . . . . **$250–$325**

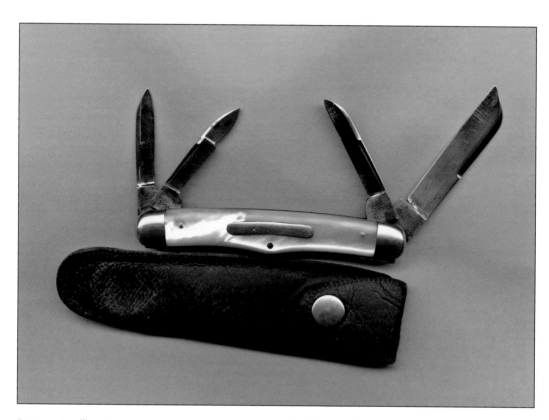

Pattern: Swell-center congress
Company: Southington Cutlery Company
Closed length: 3½"

Handle material: MOP
Value range:. . . . . **$250–$300**

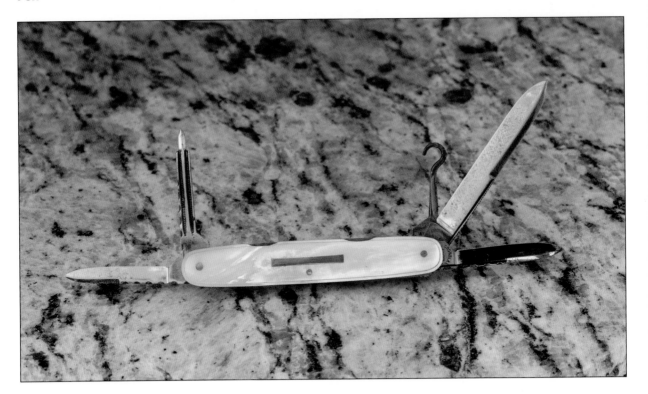

Pattern: Five-blade, equal-end pen, shadow
Company: J. Crosslands & Son
Closed length: 3¼"

Handle material: MOP
Value range:. . . . . $550–$650

Pattern: Serpentine pen, dogleg
Company: J.A. Henckels
Closed length: 3¼"

Handle material: Stag jigged bone
Value range:. . . . . **$145–$160**

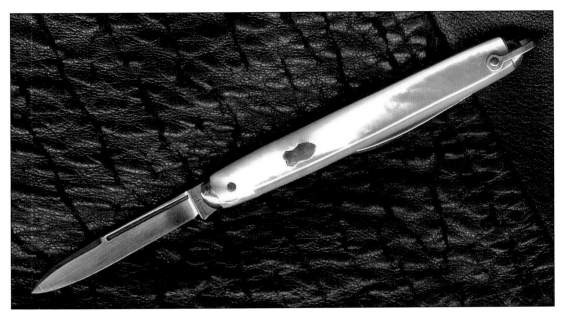

Pattern: Equal-end pen
Company: J.A. Henckels
Closed length: 2¾"

Handle material: MOP
Value range:. . . . . **$125–$135**

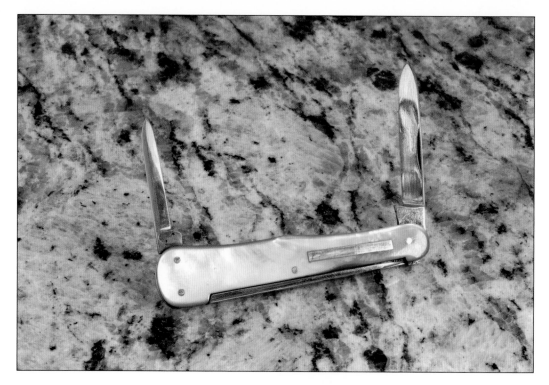

Pattern: Lobster
Pattern number: 3280
Company: New York Knife Company

Closed length: 3⅛"
Handle material: MOP
Value range:.................. **$225–$250**

Pattern: Serpentine lobster pen, "Orange
Blossom"
Company: New York Knife Company

Closed length: 3¼"
Handle material: MOP
Value range:.................. **$350–$450**

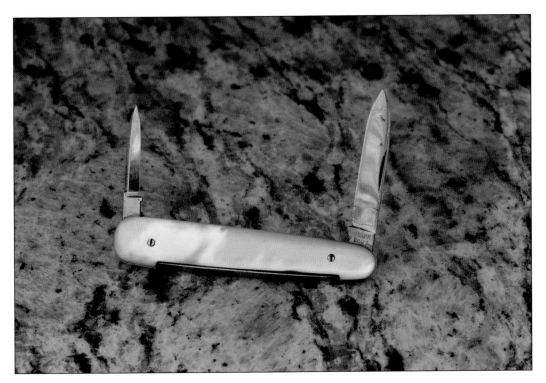

Pattern: Sleeveboard lobster pen
Company: Miller Brothers
Closed length: 3⅛"

Handle material: MOP
Value range:................... $250–$300

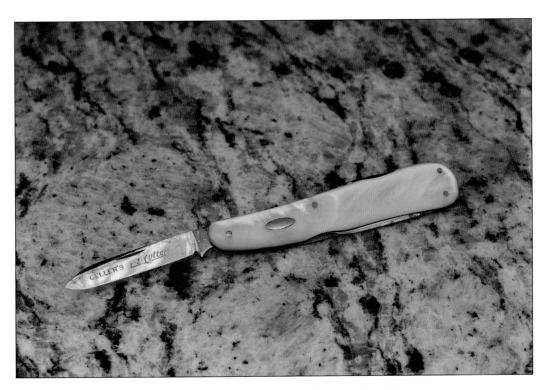

Pattern: Serpentine lobster pen
Company: American Shear & Knife Company
Closed length: 3¼"

Handle material: MOP
Value range:................... $250–$350

Pattern: Sleeveboard lobster
Company: J.A. Henckels
Closed length: 3"

Handle material: MOP
Value range:. . . . .$200–$225

Pattern: Serpentine lobster
Company: Wade & Butcher
Closed length: 3¼"

Handle material: MOP
Value range:. . . . .$200–$260

Pattern: Sheffield lobster
Company: Cattaraugus
Closed length: 2¾"

Handle material: MOP
Value range:.........................$175–$225

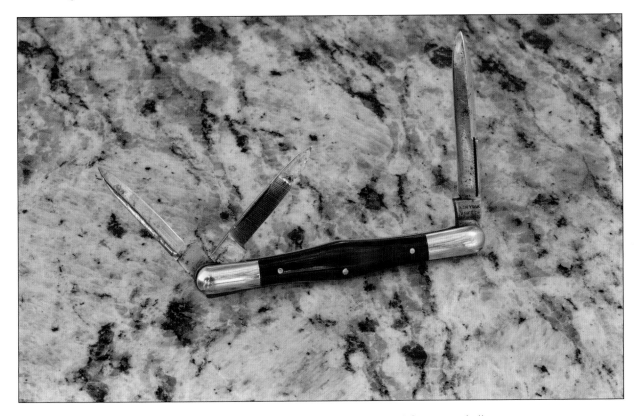

Pattern: Swell-center pen, "tuxedo"
Company: New York Knife Company
Closed length: 3"

Handle material: Tortoise shell
Value range:.........................$150–$180

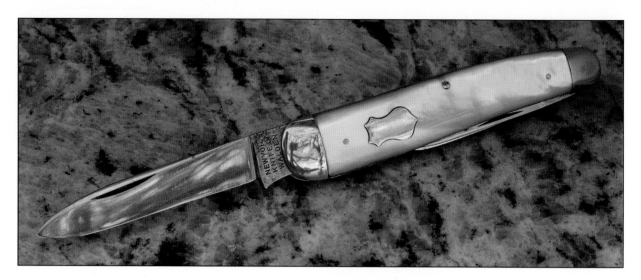

Pattern: Serpentine pen
Company: New York Knife Co., Hammer Brand
Closed length: 3¼"

Handle material: MOP
Value range:...........................**$250–$300**

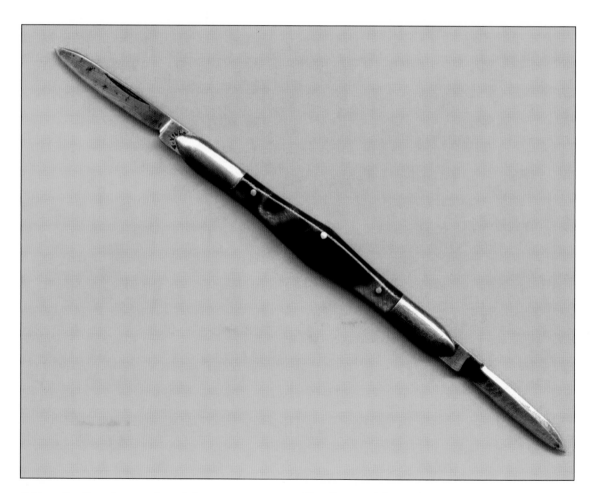

Pattern: Swell-center pen, "tuxedo"
Company: Waterville
Closed length: 3"

Handle material: Tortoise
Value range:.....................**$150–$170**

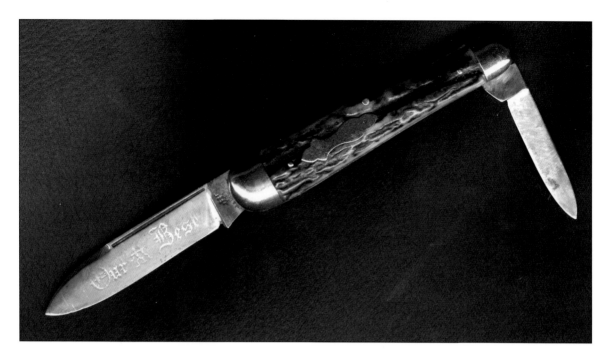

Pattern: Swell-center serpentine pen, "half whittler"
Company: J.A. Henckels
Closed length: 3⅜"

Handle material: Stag
Value range:. . . . . **$225–$250**

Pattern: Equal-end pen
Company: W.R. Humphreys & Co.
Closed length: 3¼"

Handle material: Tortoise shell
Value range:. . . . . **$70–$80**

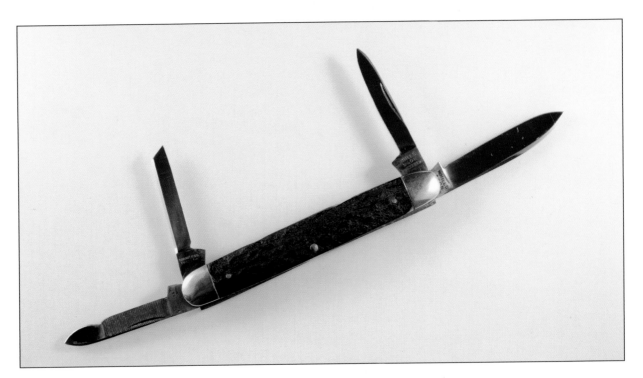

Pattern: Equal-end pen, senator
Company: W. Mills & Son
Closed length: 3½"

Handle material: Dyed stag
Value range:. . . . .**$100–$125**

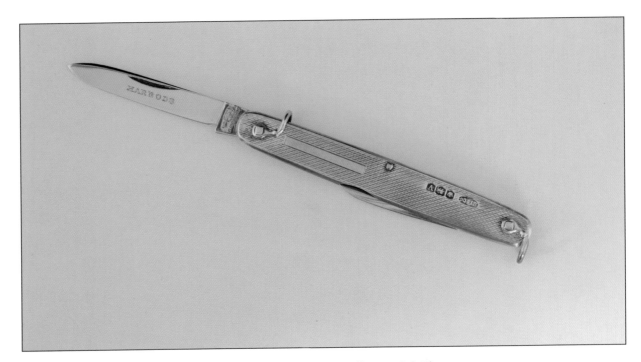

Pattern: Equal-end pen
Company: George Ibberson & Co.
Closed length: 3¼"

Handle material: Silver
Value range:. . . . .**$80–$90**

Pattern: Advertising
Pattern number: R6499
Company: Remington Arms Company

Closed length: 3"
Handle material: Metal
Value range:. . . . .**$200–$300**

Pattern: Advertising
Pattern number: Salesman's sample, 7429 etch
Company: Eagle Knife Company (Winchester store knife)

Closed length: 3⅛"
Handle material: Metal
Value range:. . . . .**$350–$450**

Pattern: Advertising
Company: Salesman's sample, 7429 etch
Closed length: 3"

Handle material: Metal
Value range:.................. $200–$300

Utility/Scout

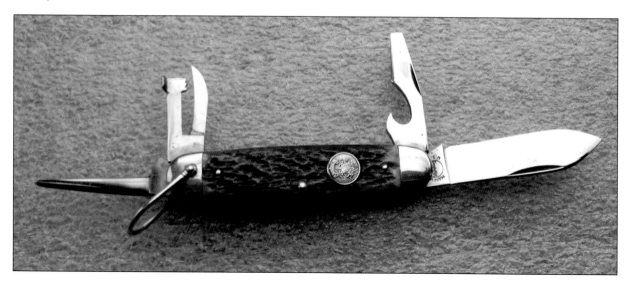

Pattern: Boy Scouts of America, utility
Pattern number: R3333
Company: Remington Arms Company

Closed length: 3⅝"
Handle material: Jigged brown bone
Value range:..........................$400–$450

Pattern: Utility
Company: Schrade Cutlery Company, Walden, New York.
Closed length: 3½"

Handle material: Peachseed jigged bone
Value range:..........................$180–200

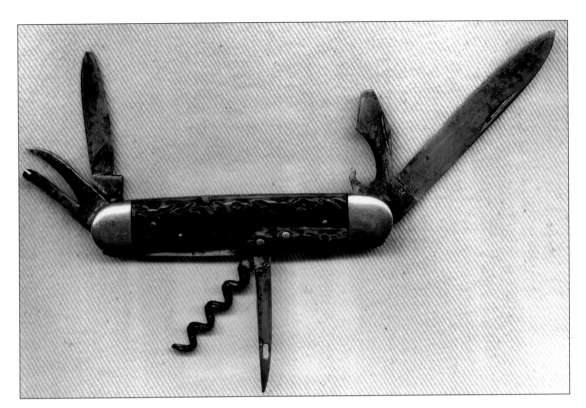

Pattern: Utility
Company: J.A. Henckels
Closed length: 3½"

Handle material: Stag
Value range:. . . . .$80–$90

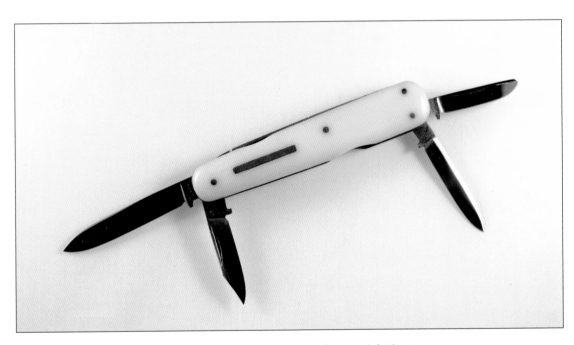

Pattern: Utility
Company: W. Mills & Son
Closed length: 3¼"

Handle material: Plastic
Value range:. . . . . $60–$70

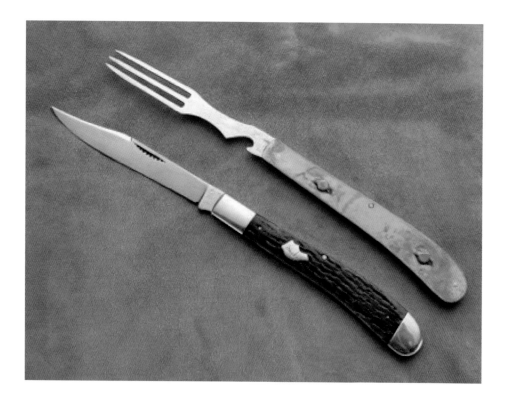

Pattern: Slot knife, commonly called "hobo" knife
Company: KA-BAR, dog's head shield
Closed length: 5¼"

Handle material: Jigged bone
Value range: . . . . $550–$600

Pattern: Slot knife, "hobo"
Company: Brookes & Crookes
Closed length: 4½"

Handle material: Stag
Value range:. . . . .**$250–$300**

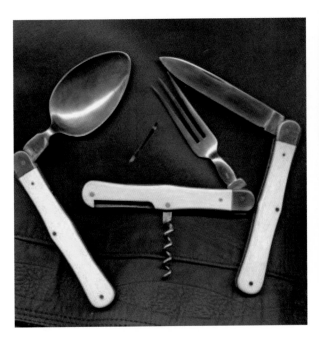

Pattern: Camping set, knife, fork, corkscrew, spoon, tortoise toothpick
Company: J.A. Henckels

Closed length: 4⅜"
Handle material: Ivory
Value range:. . . . .**$200–$225**

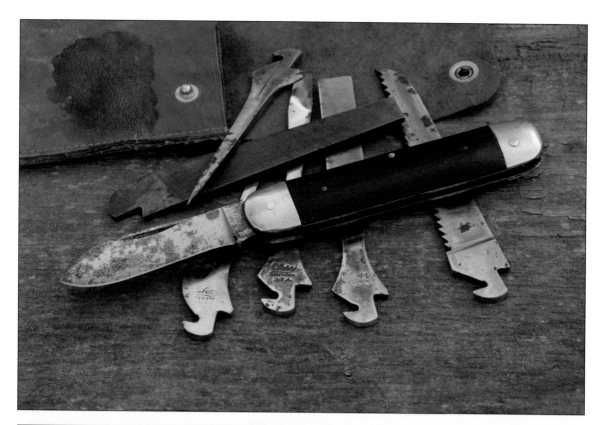

Pattern: Tool kit
Company: Ulery (made by Napanoch)
Closed length: 3¾"

Handle material: Ebony
Value range:....................... $160–$200

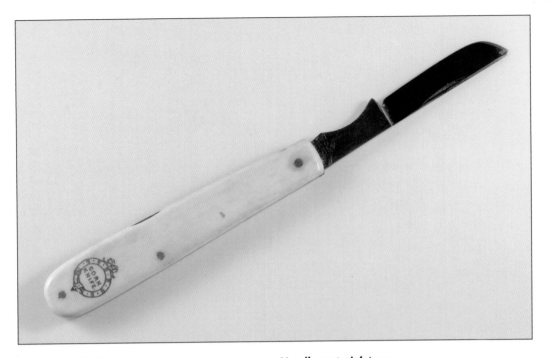

Pattern: Corn knife
Company: John Clarke & Son
Closed length: 3½"

Handle material: Ivory
Value range:. . . . . **$40–$50**

Pattern: Corn knife
Company: J.A. Henckels
Closed length: 3"

Handle material: Plastic, "French ivory"
Value range:. . . . . **$20–$30**

Pruner

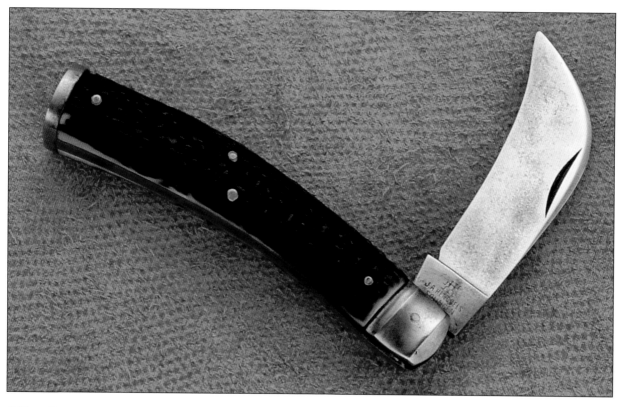

Pattern: Pruner
Company: J.A. Henckels
Closed length: 4³⁄₁₆"

Handle material: Stag
Value range:. . . . . $250–$300

Fixed blades

Pattern: Bowie
Maker: William Nicholson, Sheffield, England, circa 1850s
Full length: 12½"

Handle material: Stag
Value range:. . . . . $5,000–$6,000

Pattern: Hunting knife
Pattern number: 602
Company: J.A. Henckels, Friodur

Full length: 9¾"
Handle material: Stag
Value range:. . . . .$150–$180

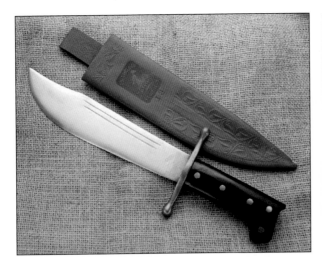

Pattern: Pilot's survival machete
Pattern number: No. 18
Company: Collins

Full length: 14"
Handle material: Black phenolic plastic
Value range:. . . . .$400–$500

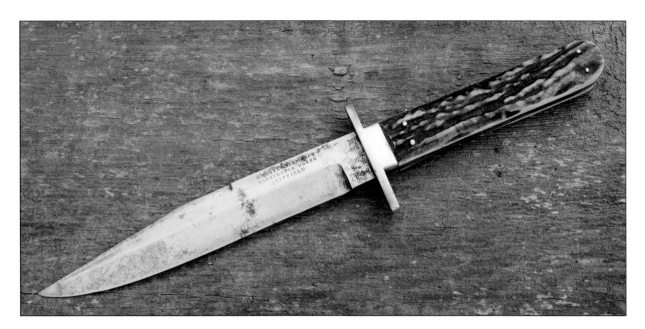

Pattern: Bowie
Company: George Wostenholm, IXL
Full length: 10⅜"

Handle material: Stag
Value range:. . . . . **$1,000-$1,300**

Miscellaneous

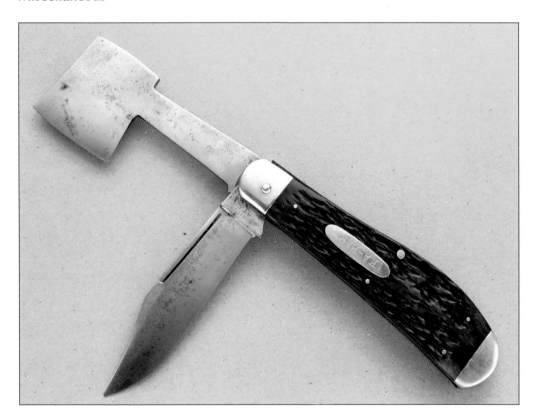

Pattern: Cherry tree chopper
Company: Union Cutlery Company, KA-BAR
Closed length: 5"

Handle material: Jigged bone
Value range:. . . . .**$750–$800**

Pattern: Carriage knife
Company: Beaver Cutlery (made by Robeson with Robeson punch patent)

Closed length: 3⅝"
Handle material: Jigged black composite
Value range:. . . . . **$800–$900**

Pattern: Dog groomer
Pattern number: R4733
Company: Remington Arms Company

Closed length: 3¾"
Handle material: Jigged brown bone
Value range:. . . . . **$400–$475**

Pattern: Radio knife
Pattern number: 632800
Company: Robeson Cutlery Company

Closed length: 3¼"
Handle material: Jigged brown bone
Value range:. . . . .**$500–$600**

Pattern: Wrench knife
Pattern number: 3-W
Company: Cattaraugus

Closed length: 4¼"
Handle material: Brown jigged bone
Value range:. . . . .**$400–$500**

Pattern: Carving set
Company: J.A. Henckels
Overall length: 4¼ knife, 14¼" with handle

Handle material: Stag
Value range:. . . . . $100–$125

X: Traditional Custom Knife Makers

While we are well past the Golden Age of cutlery that lasted roughly up to World War II, it's currently a good era to pick up a pocketknife or fixed blade from a custom knife maker.

The following profiles first appeared in *Knife World*, but other custom makers worth checking out include: Bruce Bump, Joel Chamblin, Ray Cover, Brent Cramer, Terry Davis, Bret Dowell, Steve Dunn, Don Hanson, Jerry Halfrich, Kerry Hampton, D'Alton Holder, Jess Horn, Ryuichi Kawamura, K R Johnson, Steve Johnson, John Lloyd, Takeshi Matsusaki, Don Morrow, Rick Noland, Jared Oeser, Hiroaki Ohta, Enrique Pena, Rusty Preston, Tom Overeynder, Richard Rogers, Kyle Royer, Bill Ruple, Eugene Shadley, Stan Shaw, David

Taber, C. Gray Taylor, John White, John Young, and Mike Zscherny.

(Some profiles have been revised and updated.)

Tony Bose Breathes New Life into Vintage Pocket Knives

Fortune smiled upon Tony Bose when he lost most of the vision in one of his eyes when he was six years old.

Bose's eye was hit by a friend's arrow that was made from kite sticks, and even though he lost most of the sight in his right eye, he has a slight amount of peripheral vision left. It caused him a lot of trauma early on, but Bose now jokes that he perfected the no-look pass

▲ This ivory Tony Bose saddlehorn sports damascus steel blades forged by fellow knife maker Don Hanson.

as a high school point guard because opposing teams couldn't tell where he was looking.

Bose said the arrow in the eye incident turned out to be a blessing, because his limited eyesight was considered a liability by some would-be employers.

Instead, the injury allowed Bose to sharpen his focus on making traditional pocketknives.

While there may be some who don't consider Tony Bose the best custom traditional pocketknife maker to date—Tony's son, Reese is right up there, as well—there's no debating that he has elevated the craft to a new stratosphere, and many of today's traditional customer makers stand upon Tony Bose's accomplishments.

In 2007, Bose received the Red Watson Memorial Friendship Award at the Knifemakers' Guild Show in Orlando, Florida. The award is given each year to knife makers who show a willingness to share their knowledge of knife making with their peers, and it was Bose's peers who voted to give him the award.

When he first started making knives, Bose said he asked a knife maker to share a pattern with him.

"He wouldn't give it to me," Bose said. "I thought to myself then that if anyone ever asked me for a pattern,

▲ Bose used stag from an old kitchen carving set on this two-blade teardrop jack knife.

I would give it to them, and I always have. I've sent them all over the world."

Jack Davenport is a talented knife maker in his own right, having won several best folder awards at the Blade Show. Davenport won the awards using Tony Bose's five-blade Rogers whittler pattern.

"Tony is one of the most knowledgeable men in old classic pocketknife patterns out there," Davenport said. "He has most of it right in his head, and if he doesn't have it in his head, he has it in his pattern box. He's just a fount of information when it comes to old pocketknife patterns. Every multiblade I've made so far and been recognized for has been a Tony Bose pattern that he sent to me out of the grace of his generosity."

Having collected hundreds of vintage pocketknives and traveled the National Knife Collectors Association (NKCA) circuit for years, Bose knows traditional slip-joint patterns front to back. Davenport said Bose is willing to not only share the patterns with other makers, but also discuss how the knives are made.

Bose is willing to help neophyte knife makers, as well. Kerry Hampton found out that Bose lived nearby when he looked Bose's name up in a knife reference book. Hampton called Bose and nervously blurted out that he wanted to learn how to make knives. From that cold call, Hampton has become one of the premier traditional pocketknife makers himself.

▲ Bose grinds a blade in his Wilfred Works shop on his twenty-inch Burr King grinder.

A Career is Born

Bose worked in factories and then had a union carpenter's card when he "first started foolin' around" with making knives in 1972. After many years of repairing pocketknives, Bose made two fixed blades from a friend's broken hacksaw blade.

"I've always been interested in knives ever since I was a little kid," Bose said. "I was making some straight blades and repairing pocketknives, but I finally decided if I can repair a pocketknife then I should be able to make one. Then I found it was a helluva lot harder than that."

Bose made his first pocketknife in 1975. It was a four-inch single-blade folder with a drop point that wasn't based on a traditional pattern.

He didn't join the Knifemakers' Guild for eighteen years because he "wanted to be good enough to be there and not go there and be embarrassed."

In the early going, Bose didn't have the luxury of today's equipment and technologies, nor did he have other knife makers that he could ring up for advice. He used a hard-wheel grinder that "went a gazillion miles per hour" and hand-rubbed the grind marks out.

"I just made them any way I could," he said. "I'd file them out and then do them on a hard-wheel grinder. They worked OK if you were grinding a big old camp knife but not when you're doing the pen blade on a pocketknife. When I finally got a belt grinder, I couldn't believe how much easier it could be."

Today Tony and Reese use Burr King grinders set up in different configurations around the shop. Several years ago, Bose received a prototype Burr King grinder with a twenty-inch wheel, which he now uses for most of his blade grinding.

"The hardest thing to learn to do is grind, and then predict what you're going to grind and do it again," Bose said. "I tell aspiring knife makers that that the first thing you have to have is a real bad case of the 'want tos,' because if you don't really want to do it, you'll give up before you get good at it.

"The other thing is if you're going to make traditional knives, you need to know what they're supposed to look like. I see guys that make something that looks like an inbred cat. It just doesn't look right. The best thing anyone can do is go to antique knife shows and pick 'em up and study 'em to see what was done in the past."

▲ A serpentine wharncliffe trapper by Tony Bose.

As an avid hunter, Bose wore down many a Case trapper skinning squirrels and rabbits since he likes to keep the blades "hair-splitting sharp." Bose said he didn't have much use for the spey blade, so he would grind it down into a muskrat blade.

In the mid-1980s, Bose came up with one of his most popular patterns, the two-blade wharncliffe trapper in which the wharncliffe blade takes the place of the spey blade.

Over the years, Bose also carried a Case folding hunter in his back pocket next to his wallet because he didn't like the way belt sheaths hung on things. Bose modified a Remington 1123 pattern for his back pocket knife. It comes in four- and four-and-a-half-inch sizes, the latter of which has a square and clean joint.

"I do more wharncliffe trappers and back pocket knives than anything else, and the reason I do is because they just work," said Bose, who is also known as the Old Dog. "They're useful knives. I wish every knife I made was in somebody's pocket going to work."

Bose said he was doing a pretty good job of making knives in the 1980s, but he really started hitting his stride when he went full time in 1990.

"It was a big step to quit a job and do this full time, but I just kept getting orders," he said. "I talked to my wife, and I said, 'If you could do this, wouldn't you want to?' It was into the 1990s before I started getting enough money out of them that I could make a living out of knife making."

Reese Bose, who had a knife sharpening business starting in the third grade, joined his father in the workshop in 1993.

A Case for a Collaboration

Today, Bose knives can typically sell for more than twice or even three times what Tony and Reese charge for them. Aside from winning a Bose knife at the annual Blade Show drawing, getting a Bose knife quickly usually requires paying high dollar amounts to knife dealers. Reese's customer wait list is more than five years, and Tony no longer accepts orders.

Of course, it wasn't always high-cotton in the early days of grinding knives in the shop, but as Tony Bose's knives became the standard for traditional slipjoints, a large company came calling.

Knife World Editor Mark Zalesky was at the W.R. Case and Sons Cutlery Company factory in 1998 when he was asked if he knew of any good custom knife makers who made traditional patterns. Zalesky recommended Tony Bose, and a month later the knife maker met with Case officials at a knife show to discuss a collaboration. That meeting resulted in the first Tony Bose/Case collaboration knife, which was a slimline trapper.

From there, a mutually beneficial relationship was born that continues to this day.

"It made my life a hell of lot easier, is what it did," Bose said. "When you collaborate with someone, you draw royalties off of it. Before that, whenever I used to get ready for shows it would be two months without a paycheck because I was laying everything back for the show. But now I don't have to worry as much because I get royalties from them. It made my life a lot easier."

Rich Brandon, Case's Engineering Manager, said Tony refers to his association with Case as his 401k.

For its part, Case has been able to tap into Tony Bose's wealth of knowledge on making pocketknives.

"He's always been a wonderful source of knowledge for us," Brandon said. "The biggest thing I've enjoyed with Tony over the years, other than him just being a good ol' boy, is that he won't hide anything from you. If you ask him a question, he'll tell you exactly what he believes is the best way to do something. He's not arrogant about something being a proprietary process, and that's a tremendous learning experience not only for myself but also for a lot of our manufacturing folks over the years.

"He's often told me that if he can keep me from making the mistakes that he made, he's more than willing to do that."

Bose is known to walk the production floor at Case and hob knob with employees about how the knives are made. Brandon said Bose has showed Case employees knife-making techniques that extend beyond the Bose/Case collaborations and into the production line. In 1995, Bose started using bushings in his knives on the advice of another knife maker. Case now uses bushings in several of its production models, including the copperlock.

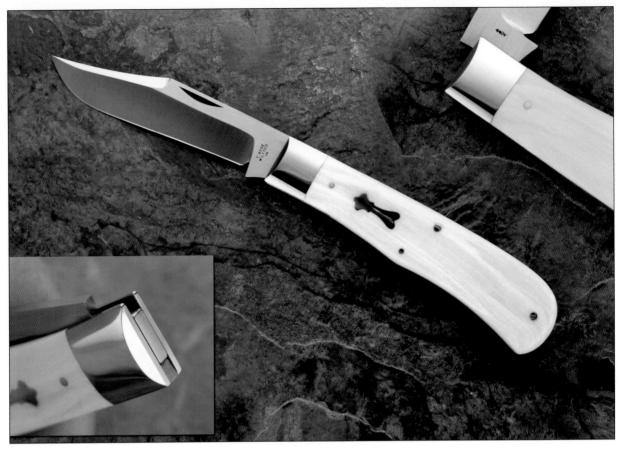

▲ This 4 ½-inch Bose saddleback features square and clean construction in the tang and backspring.

"Sometimes I think they're not listening to me, but I end up seeing it in what they're doing," Bose said. "They treat me like an Olympic champion."

Bose currently makes forty to fifty knives a year because of his commitment to attend Case events and work with Brandon's team on collaborations.

Tony Bose said the hardest knives to make are the five and six-blade pocketknives, as well as the lockback whittler. Brandon said Case was especially proud that it made a lockback whittler one year as the Bose/Case collaboration.

What Makes a Bose a Bose

Aside from using some of the best handle materials and the seemingly flawless fit and finish on the knives, there are several characteristics of a Bose knife. While Tony Bose certainly didn't invent swedges on knife blades, he did breathe new life into them. Bose credits the turn of the century knife makers from Sheffield for his and Reese's swedgework on the blades.

"I tell a lot of people that we don't design knives, we bring them back from the grave," Bose said. "When you look at a lot of the old Sheffield knives, they had real prominent swedge work on them, but then they died off and the Depression came, so you didn't hardly see any swedges on a slipjoint. It's a type of grinding that was pretty well lost by the 1960s."

Bose said grinding a swedge was the hardest part of making a knife, and even Reese went through a learning curve while "bellying up" to the grinder.

"It's not for the faint of heart; I'll tell you that," he said. "My jigs for that are hanging right on the end of my wrists. It's all hand-ground, but you have to develop a feel for it. I think that kind of separates Reese and me from the other makers, because they'll do swedgework, but they won't do it as boldly."

Bose is also known for the fluted bolsters on his knives, which hark back to how traditional pocket-knives used to be made.

▲ An original KA-BAR dog's head trapper, top, and the Tony Bose custom version.

"Fluted bolsters is kind of a trademark of mine," Bose said. "In the past, they were done a lot and were called rattail bolsters. Mine are a little longer because on a Remington the pivot pin is in the flute, and you can always see them, which I don't want to happen. I make them a little longer, so the pin won't be in the flute, and I can get it to mesh where you can't see it."

The Boses jig some of their own bone or use vintage Napanoch or Remington bone. On a KA-BAR dog's head knife, they re-create the original feather jigging pattern. They also heat treat some of the steel they use.

The Old Dog Keeps His Nose to the Grindstone

Bose, who turned 68 in 2014, is in the twilight of his knife-making career, but he's still looking for new challenges.

Bose said he wished more of his knives were used instead of becoming collector's pieces sitting in safes. He points out that most people don't have a problem driving a new BMW after purchasing one, so they shouldn't feel reluctant to use one of his knives.

"If I'm ever remembered for anything after I'm gone, I hope they say 'Those things really cut' instead of how pretty or how well-done they are," he said. "I want to keep doing this until I die and grind a quarter-inch of my nose away on one of those Burr Kings. I want to keep doing it as long as I can, but Father Time will have a way of making me quit."

These days, Bose said his back gets a little sore when he's grinding all five blades in one day for a multi-blade knife, and then there's the strain on his good left eye, but the Old Dog still has a few new tricks left. His legacy will last until the last Bose knife disappears from the planet.

"Most people don't remember past their grandparents, but one hundred years from now, someone will see a knife with 'T. Bose, Wilfred, Indiana' on it, and that will be my legacy," he said.

▲ A stockman pattern with punch blade by Tony Bose.

Tony Bose Speaks

- "Chicken eye and coon fingering" is a term Tony and Reese Bose coined. It can apply to knives, knife materials, guns, or just about anything else that deserves an up close and personal inspection from several angles.

- "I know some of [my knives] go for crazy prices, but I wish more people would use them," he said. "It's cut first; everything else is bells and whistles. I'm proud of the way I can do it, but I'm more proud of how they cut.

- "I like to make things that you can't go down to the hardware store and buy now, patterns that are interesting. I've never made a liner-lock in my life.

- "I don't have any trouble with motivation and neither does Reese. I work every day. The reason I work every day is because that's what buys the groceries. My motivation is buying groceries. It's hard work, but I've never been able to leave it alone.

- "[New knife makers] are a legend in their own minds after reading about themselves. Myself, when I come home from the Blade Show I have a little woman here who takes care of any ego problems that may have come up while I was gone.

- "I work at not having an ego and not thinkin' I'm special, because we're not curing cancer here. It's just a pocketknife."

Todd Davison Carves His Own Path

Traditional pocketknife maker Todd Davison is a rebel with a cause.

Davison has the gruff timbre of cowboy actor Sam Elliott, and when he's not making pocketknives, he likes to ride his Harley. He's a self-made knife maker that likes to do things his own way. Unlike most makers, Davison doesn't use patterns when he makes a pocketknife.

"I don't have any patterns," he said. "I've had guys call me and ask for patterns, and I tell them I can make them one that is close, but I don't have patterns. That's just the way I learned how to do it. I drill a hole in a piece of steel, and that's where I start at. A lot of people say it's the wrong way and that I should use patterns, but to me a true custom knife is your own design.

"A lot of the knife guys kind of dogged me out and have made me the dark sheep because I don't use

▲ Davison uses a lot of stabilized wood on his knives, including the black and gold box elder on this knife.

patterns. Some of them seem to kind of frown on me for not following suit. I just try to do the best I can, and really the guys who are building knives, they're the ones that are doing it every day. They know what works and what doesn't work and what is the best and what isn't the best."

Davison was Self-Taught

Growing up in Mississippi, Davison used knives for hunting and fishing and eventually ran across another custom knife maker.

"They were kind of crude, but they were cool to me," he said. "It just amazed me, and I came home and bought a bunch of stuff and thought I'd try it."

Davison didn't have a lot of help in the early days of his fixed-blade career, but he did come across the name and number of another knife maker in a knife magazine, which at least led to some tips over the phone.

"I picked up a *Blade* magazine, and I was looking for someone to talk to and ask questions," he said. "It just so happened that when I got that magazine there was a guy in there with his phone number. I called him up and asked him a million questions, and guess who it turned out to be? It was (custom fixed-blade knife legend) Bob Loveless. I called him and starting asking all of these questions, and I didn't have a clue who he was.

"He was always nice to me. He never told me he was too busy, and he laughed at me for some of the things that I was doing or trying to do. He set me straight, and after all of these years, I finally figured out who he was."

After periodically making fixed-blade knives part-time for several decades, Davison started making traditional pocketknives in 2002 and then went full time in 2008. Davison said he started out by taking old pocketknives apart and putting them back together. He also consulted vintage knife catalogs and studied traditional patterns.

"After I got to where I could put them back together, I started making the pieces and parts and tried to put them together," he said. "I kept trying to make them better. Tony Bose helped me a whole lot. I got to where I could make a pocketknife, but I really didn't know the specifics of how everything was supposed to work, the fit and finish it was supposed to have, the action, the grinds. The perfection came from Tony Bose.

"He's the one that really helped me, and he's helped a lot of others, as well. I've called Tony Bose so many times that I was expecting him to say 'Todd, don't call me anymore,' or tell me he was just too busy, but he never did. He always took the time. It didn't matter, he would answer every question I ever had the best he could."

Wood and Micarta Handles

Davison has made all manner of pocketknives, but is primarily known for his single-blade knives with micarta and wood scales.

"I make a swayback, but I make mine by either looking at a picture or it's something that I make up myself," he said. "I can look at a picture of a knife and make it by the picture. A knife I make may look like the one I made before, but I never drew it up from the last one to put on the next one, so it's all brand new. I think that's a little more unique."

While Davison can make a knife with any handle material, he favors the strength and utility of micarta scales. Davison came up with his own striper micarta scales as a way of setting himself apart from the crowd and to add a little color to work.

"Micarta is the strongest material there is, but I thought I would try to make a pretty micarta knife," Davison said. "They used to make those candy stripe knives, and then you had ol' Bill Scagel that made a lot of knives with stripes on them. I was trying to make the best knife I could and make the prettiest knife out of the strongest material. Those stripes in the handles, across the bottom of them just barely above the bottom of the micarta, there's two 1/16-inch pins that run the full length of the handle underneath there, and they're pinned together and then pinned to the liner so they can't ever come out."

Davison also likes to use stabilized wood from Wood Stabilizing Specialists International on his knives.

"I think it's just really super stuff," he said. "They used to use wood on a lot of the old pocketknives, but some of them would crack and break. This stuff I use now is penetrated all the way through, and it polishes

◀ This single-blade knife features fluted bolsters and amber worm jigged bone.

◀ A striper pattern by Davison with pinned micarta stripes and wood scales.

out good and seals real well. I'm trying to make them last a long time, and I'm just trying to build the best knife that I can."

Davison will use stag, jigged bone, elephant ivory, and mammoth ivory for handle scales if that's what a customer wants. His knife blades ran the gamut from the traditional wharncliffes, spear, clip, and drop points to a utility razor. His models include trappers, swaybacks, and other assorted jack knifes. He has also made two-bladed, three-bladed, and four-bladed knives.

In the Shop

Davison heat-treats his blades in his shop in Lyons, Kansas, and the blades are hollow ground on a grinder.

"I do my own heat treating, and I test every one of them," Davison said. "For all of my stainless steel, I try

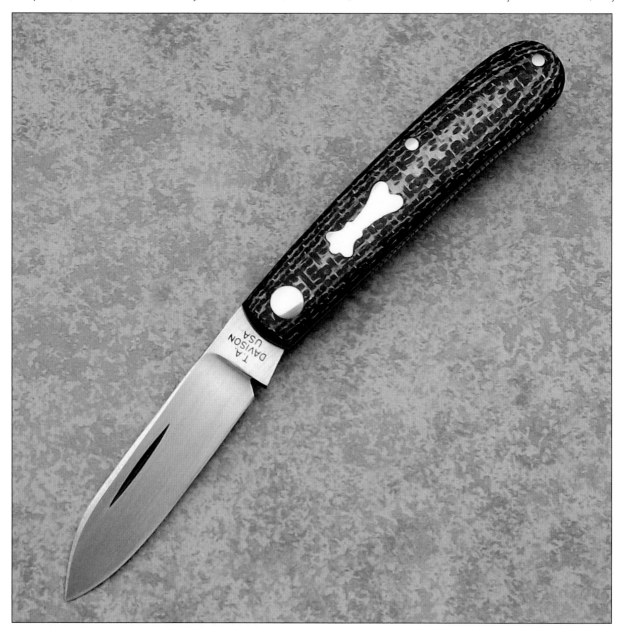

▲ A single-blade shadow pattern with blue and silver twill scales.

to get them between 60 and 61 Rockwell. Sometimes it's between 61 and 62, and I do a cryogenic quench on them, so it raises them a point or two.

"I use 410 stainless for the liners and bolsters, and for blade stock, I use a little bit of everything. I use a lot of ATS-34, D2, and CPM 154. I've used about everything that there is. I can pretty much make it out of anything they want."

If a customer wants a high polish on a blade, Davison said he tries to steer them away from S30V, and if it's going to be a user knife, he'll suggest a belt finish.

Aside from his phone calls with Loveless and Bose, Davison said he's only stepped foot into one other knife maker's shop, which was Rick Menefee's shop in Oklahoma.

▲ This wharncliffe blade is paired with G-10 scales and a double-bomb shield. Davison stamps a number inside of each knife he makes.

"I've talked to Menefee on the telephone, and we both decided that when you are learning how to make slip joints, it's suicidal," he said. "You work on a knife for three days just to tear it apart and throw it away. There's just so much in there. The hardest thing for me was to learn how to hide that (pivot) pin in the bolsters, which is usually hard for everybody. I've had several knife makers call me to try to figure out how to do that. It's not easy to do.

"There's a lot to making those knives. A lot of people just don't know what really goes on with making a pocketknife. There are just so many things that make a difference. Everything you do makes you do something else different."

Each one of Davison's knives has a number stamped inside of the liner, and he has numbered every pocketknife he has made. As of 2014, Davison had topped the one thousand mark with his numbered knives. When he finishes a knife, he writes down the number, what kind of knife it is, the type of shield and scales, the length closed, and the date it was made, all of which makes it easier for a new or old customer to order a similar knife from him.

▲ The orange G-10 scales on this knife are hard to miss in just about any setting. One of Davison's trademarks is filework on the inside of the mirror-finished liners.

"I've known his dad for a long time, and he actually gave me knife number one hundred," said Jim Reavis, a knife collector in Pueblo, Colorado. "I've gotten all of his two hundred, three hundred, four hundred, five hundred, and up knives to date, and I've ordered them all the way through one thousand. They're quality knives and the craftsmanship has definitely improved from one hundred to nine hundred.

"He is quite the character. He's one of a kind. He's done bronc riding, trained horses, and he's done a lot of other things. He's just a quality down-to-earth good American. His word is his bond."

Aside from numbering each knife, Davison also uses a chainsaw file to put filework on the inside of his springs.

"I started off doing that because of the way I cut the spring. When I started, I didn't have any way to get a good finish in there," he said. "I didn't have a machine to get up into those curves to give me the finish that I wanted. So started doing that so I could put a mirror finish and to make it as perfect as I could down in there. I've done it on every one of them.

"I can get more of a precision finish in there, plus it kind of gives me a little better way to adjust the tension on those springs. With a mirror finish, it reflects off of the liners, so when you look down in there it's really lit up instead of dark."

He has also sold a lot of linerless micarta or G-10 shadow knives, which are both durable and lightweight.

One advantage of Davison's free wheelin' knife-making ways is that he can implement changes on the fly when he is making a knife. He said he's always trying to think of ways to make a better knife or to make something different than what the rest of the knife maker herd is doing.

"Ever since I started making pocket knives, I've gone ten or twelve hours every day hard," he said. "Most people hate their jobs, but I get up out of bed

▲ A stag swayback by Rick Menefee with premium stag scales.

and instead of sitting there and drinking coffee, I grab my coffee and take it out to the shop. I'm ready to go. I love it, and you've really got to because learning how to make those things takes some time.

"This is about all I do. I got a Harley, and I go ride it every once a while. I take a trip down to Mississippi to see my kids, but other than that, I really don't have any other hobbies. I'm either making knives or taking a short trip on my Harley to see my kids. That clears my mind and relieves all of the stress. When I get back, I'm ready to go. I'm always thinking of how I can make a better knife or a different knife."

Traditional Pocket Knives by Oklahoma Maker Rick Menefee

Rick Menefee is an amalgam of custom knife maker ingredients—including talent, drive, humility, and experience with a dash of redneck humor thrown in for good measure all these traits have him on the verge of joining an elite circle of knife makers.

Menefee doesn't have to look too far for inspiration when he's making traditional pocketknives in his Blanchard, Oklahoma, shop, because there's usually fifteen to twenty vintage knives on his bench and a stack of old knife catalog reprints nearby.

Menefee started making traditional pocketknives in 2005, but he has come a long way since then, and he'll be the first to tell you that he still has a long way to go. His passion for pocketknives started when he was a kid.

"My granddad was really heavy into old Schrade and Case knives," Menefee said. "I was six or seven years old when he started giving me those knives. It kind of piqued my interest, and it has just stayed with me ever since. I love traditional slipjoints. I made some fixed blades when I was a little kid. I'd buy kits and put them together. I was probably ten years old when I started doing that, and it just kind of continued. I probably ground my first blades on a real knife grinder eighteen or nineteen years ago."

Early Start With Fixed Blades

Menefee spent years making fixed blades, but in the back of his mind he always knew he would make traditional pocketknives. Like a baseball player in

▲ Menefee still makes some fixed-blade knives, including these hunting models with sheaths by Larry Parsons.

the minor leagues, he honed his craft grinding fixed blades, which also included grinding blades for supply houses.

Menefee was learning to be a knife maker on his own while also holding down his day job as a federal trapper for the USDA. Menefee, who graduated from college with a degree in wildlife conservation and wildlife law enforcement, knows firsthand what makes a knife perform well in the field from his work as a trapper.

"I had read some books early on, and when I first started with the government, I was pretty poor," he said. "I saved for about a year for my first grinding machine, and after I got that then I probably ground knives for a year and never really produced anything.

"I really didn't know anybody, and I was just trying to grind on my own. I started figuring out that there were other knife makers around that did this stuff."

One of Menefee's earliest mentors for fixed blades was George Englebretson, who lived in Oklahoma City. Englebretson helped Menefee with the fixed-blades and also introduced him to Dan Burke, who is an award-winning traditional pocketknife maker in

his own right. Menefee wanted to start making traditional pocketknives, but the school of hard knocks for fixed blades came first, including "ruining enough stag to make you want to vomit."

"I've worked with my hands my whole life, and I've built lot of things, but I needed to get to a certain point before I could build a slipjoint," he said. "There are more mechanics with slipjoints, and they're more intriguing to me. I've made so many fixed blades that it just got to be second nature. I'm not saying it's easy, but it just didn't fascinate me. There is only so much you can do with them.

"With slipjoints, when I got to the point where I could grind really nice, thin blades like little pen blades, then I started to pursue it. I spent probably a year before I made my first one, because I was trying to figure out some of the problems I was fixing to start having before I even made one."

Fellow Makers Ease Early Learning Curve

Menefee also commiserated with Todd Davison and Bret Dowell, who were pretty much on the same trajectory at the time with building traditional pocketknives.

▲ Menefee makes a wide variety of knife patterns with various blade configurations.

"The same problems were going through at the same time for all of us," Menefee said. "Todd Davidon has heard me throw fits like a two-year-old baby. The way I looked at it, if I found a problem I tried to attack it and do the best I could do on it."

He also got more direct help from Dan Burke, who at the time also lived in Oklahoma.

"Rick has really come a long way, and I'm real proud that I was able to help some," Burke said. "Whether everybody wants to admit it or not, slipjoints are the most difficult knives to make without question. There are all kinds of guys out there who say they want to do this, and then when it gets a little bit difficult they throw up their hands and do something else.

"Rick's real determined. I think that in time Rick will be one of the top makers in the United States. He has that kind of desire, and that's what it takes. It takes talent and a lot of hard work, but Rick has got that ability. He's an Oklahoma redneck, but he's a first-class guy. If he tells you something, you can take it to the bank."

Menefee also received knife patterns from Burke, as well as from Tony Bose. He said he currently has sixty to seventy patterns, which also include some of his own patterns. Burke introduced Menefee to Bose.

"I talk to both of them weekly, and they're just a wealth of information," Menefee said. "If I have a problem, I can call either of them. They're an unlimited resource, and they never ask for anything. I can call either one of them, and they'll tell me whatever I need to know. I'm fortunate.

"Some of these older guys, guys like Gary Crowder and Gerald Nichols, pioneered the new high-end materials, the equipment, and stuff like that. They had a lot of it already figured out before I started. They took probably ten or fifteen years off the learning curve for me, because I already knew what I needed to Rockwell the springs at or how to use fly cutters to cut nail nicks in with. I listened to everything that they said."

Slipjoint Making Goes into Full Swing

So with his vintage knives, catalogs, and the likes of Bose and Burke in his corner, Menefee started making traditional pocketknives, mainly single-blade shadow patterns with micarta scales for the first few years.

▲ Knife pieces and parts on Menefee's workbench in his shop in Blanchard, Oklahoma.

Menefee liked making the single-blade patterns, because they were good using knives, but Burke pushed him to aim higher.

"Rick really likes shadow patterns, and for a working knife they're excellent, but I said 'Rick, if you're going to sell knives to collectors, the guy who buys shadow patterns is probably going to buy one or two, and that's probably going to be it,'" Burke said. "Guys who buy a lot of knives want different patterns, and you have to step up to the next level and the next level and the next level.

"Rick is really good about that. He reaches. Not everyone continues to reach. They find a soft easy spot, and that's where they stay, but Rick really is aggressive about trying to get to the next level, and that's why I think Rick will eventually be one of the premier knife makers. He's got a ways to go, but it takes a while to get to get there."

Over the past few years, Menefee has stepped up his knife-making game. His lineup now includes stockman, dogleg jacks, trappers, sowbellies, fixed-blade kitchen knives, and fixed-blade hunting knives.

"One of the hardest patterns for me, for some reason, are the teardrops, because getting everything symmetrical from side to side is tough," he said. "Those smaller knives, you take off a little material here or there, and it changes things a lot more. I made some lobster knives, and they were the toughest ones I've ever made."

He has a stash of Utica and Remington bone, and he can jig and dye his own bone scales when he needs to for a bigger pattern. He also has stag, ebony, and mammoth ivory scale material, and while customers can order whatever they want, he prefers micarta.

"I've used it all, including pearl, but for me the best handle material is micarta," he said. "No doubt. I can take a hammer out to the shop and hit a piece of stag or bone, and it will fly into a thousand pieces. I can take a sledgehammer and beat that micarta all day. Moisture, humidity—it's not sensitive to anything. It doesn't shrink. It's wonderful stuff."

Menefee said he mainly uses 154 CM steel on his blades, as well as some D2 and ATS-34. The springs

▲ A 4½-inch back pocket pattern with antique micarta scales and a black Bakelite shield.

are made out of 154 CM, while the blades and springs Rockwell at 59 and 50, respectively

The majority of his hollow-ground blades come with polished belt finishes, but customers can also request hand-finishes. The tangs are stamped with Menefee Made, and the blades are cryogenic-triple tempered.

After buying his first Burr King grinder, Menefee proceeded to make five more grinders to use in his shop. He's been known to have all five running at once as he goes from belt to belt to grind and finish knives.

"Basically everything in my shop but that Burr King I've built or rebuilt," he said. "The milling machines, metal lathes—I would tear them completely down, take every nut and bolt out of them, and then rebuild them like they came out of the showroom floor. Then once I got that done, I would use those machines to make more machines."

Menefee has an assortment of shields that he makes on a pantograph mill, which he also uses to inlet the shields he crafts using two other machines.

It's a family affair in Menefee's shop. His younger brother, Rocky, makes knives, and his daughters, McKenzie and Ryen, help in the shop. His wife, Barbara, is an art teacher who keeps a close eye on his work.

"She lays it out right quick if something doesn't look right," he said. "She can see lines and how things flow, and she handles every knife I make."

When not in his shop or at his other job as a government trapper, Menefee likes to spend time with his family and compete in long-range shooting sports, as well as go hunting and fishing.

Menefee said when he first started making traditional pocketknives, he wasn't even sure if a knife would come out right before he was done. He has more peace of mind now, but he said he wanted to continue on the learning curve with better mechanics, finishes, and more elaborate patterns.

Tony Bose said that while talent was important, a truly successful knife maker needs to have a bad case of the "want tos," and that Menefee has that ingredient.

"To start, I think Rick Menefee is a real deal guy," Bose said. "I think he was born with that knife gene that I've got and that some others have got where he just really

likes them. He calls once a while with a problem, and I tell him what I think he should do to fix it. I will say this for him, he is a really good listener. He takes advice easily, and he takes criticism easily. If you see something you think he should do and you tell him about it, he doesn't get all bowed up like a tomcat.

"Rick's goals were similar to mine. He's not interested in being a big dog. Anytime you're interested in that, you're probably not going to be one because that just comes with time. I think he's a pretty good maker, and I think he's going to be around for a while."

Knife Maker Ken Coats' Dye is Cast

Inspiration can come from the most unlikely places. For traditional knife maker Ken Coats, that "aha" moment came when he saw the bones his Labrador retriever had left scattered in his backyard.

Coats, who lives in Stevens Point, Wisconsin, was in the process of discussing handle options on a fixed-blade with a customer many years ago when he noticed the large beef bones he bought at the supermarket for his dog. Both Coats and the customer agreed that the stag scales that were going to go on the knife weren't working, so they were casting about for other ideas.

"I ground the blade and then handled it out of one of those dog bones," Coats recalled. "The slabs were big enough that I could make scales for a four-and-a-half-inch drop-point hunter. The customer was happy with it, but I noticed some grease spots. That bugged me at the time; so then it began. I started to dye bone."

After dabbling in fixed blades for years, Coats started making traditional pocketknives about nine years ago. What really sets his work apart is his jigged and dyed bone.

Coats said he called fellow knife maker Terry Davis after reading the book that Davis cowrote with Eugene Shadley, but mainly his dyed bone, like the rest of his knife making, was self taught.

Coats is Known for His Dyed Bone Scales

Coats found that cow bone needed some type of oil in it to avoid dry and chalky spots and to help the dyes set.

▲ Ken Coats has spent years working on his dyed and jigged bone.

"I cut out a slab of bone, grind my radiuses in it, and then jig it," Coats said. "Then I'll put it under a vacuum with either xylene or gasoline and leave it over night. If you can get xylene or gasoline into the bone, the dye will grab it."

Coats' colors for his dyed bone runs the gamut, including brown, red, green, and blue, but after attending a knife show in Janesville, Wisconsin, one year, he remarked to his wife, Kay, that if he took thirty knives to a show, twenty-nine of them had better be brown bone.

"From what I gather, some of the top people in the industry are seeking his advice on his dyes, because he really has the process nailed," said Mike Houlihan, who has been collecting Coats knives for years. "It's not an easy process to master. It's a whole science within itself, but somehow he has done enough experimentation to have it figured out."

Before dying the bone, Coats checks for trans-lucency on each set of scales by holding them up to an incandescent light. He makes sure that each scale in a set has the same level of translucency and also checks for chalky spots. Coats uses a variety of dyes on his scales, including Fiebings' oil-based leather dyes, as well as aniline dye powders cut with denatured alcohol and mixed with xylene.

"It's been a very, very long process," Coats said. "I've tried to teach a lot of people, but there are so many complicated areas of dying bone and stuff that will give you trouble. I'm just now to a point where I'm happy with it."

Old Slaughterhouse Provides More Material

Coats' obsession with bone included tramping around the Wisconsin River after the river was drawn down to its lowest levels in roughly eighty years. In addition to finding a horse's femur, he also found all manner of animal bones near the former location of a slaughterhouse.

▲ A dog's head shield is inlet into the jigged bone scales on this knife by Ken Coats.

"That afternoon, a friend of mine and myself took off for a point on the other side of the river where we heard the slaughterhouse was, and we came back with a gunnysack full of cow, sheep, and horse leg bones," Coats said. "It was kind of cool, because a lot of it looked like mammoth bark ivory. Some of it had a very crackled look, and it even had coloration like mammoth. Most of this stuff was in four to six feet of water for more than eighty years. I used a fair amount of it, but I still have some left that I had cleaned up for smaller scales."

For jigging bone, Coats makes one-inch rotary cutting tools with eight points out of ATS-34 steel with his Dremel.

"I can remember seeing Ken jig a bone handle," said Houlihan. "For some reason I thought it would take forever, but he zipped right through it. His jigging patterns have become more varied and more refined. He can look at something and know exactly how to reproduce it."

A Lifelong Fascination with Knives

Like most knife makers, Coats has had a long-time fascination with knives. He started using his high school biology scalpels for cleaning brook trout, and when he joined the Air Force, he ground his own scalpels out of bolts.

Coats continued to "mess around with knives" after he left the Air Force, and he attended his first Guild Show in Kansas City in 1972. While working as a mechanic, painter, or other jobs, he bought blades from Bob Schrimsher to make fixed blades, but Coats itched to do more.

"Around 1977, I decided I'd never be happy until I made my own blades," he said. "I bought my first

▲ A swayback jack with cap bolsters and stabilized maple wood scales.

Olympic square-wheel grinder back then, and it's still running in my shop today."

Houlihan said that Coats forged his own steel for a bit before deciding his time could be better spent by making more knives via stock removal. Around 2000, Coats made his first folding pocketknife.

"I'm almost completely self-taught," he said. "There was Shadley's and Davis' book, but back then it was so far over my head that I just started taking old junker knives from knife shows apart and it went from there. In fact, the very first junker I took apart from a knife show was an Imperial toothpick, and I still use that as my toothpick pattern today.

"It was all 'by guess and by golly' back then," he said. "I was so ecstatic when I got my first folder to work."

Coats has been on a steady learning curve ever since he made that first pocketknife. He joined the Knifemakers' Guild in 2006 and won a best new maker award at the show in Orlando that same year. Two years later, he became a full voting member of the Guild. Along with Shadley, Coats said that Tom Overeynder has also helped him with his knife making.

If a customer requests it, Coats will build a pattern based on a traditional knife, such as Case's Texas Jack, but most of the patterns are his own variations on traditional knives.

"I add two or three patterns a year, but sometimes those are variations on the patterns I already have," Coats said. "If I have a pattern that worked really well, whether it's super traditional or not, I make and heat treat a pattern out of ATS-34 stock."

Sole Authorship Knives

Coats mainly uses ATS-34 steel for his blades, but he also has some 440-C, 01, D2, Damascus, and 5160 on hand if that's what a customer wants.

▲ Coats used antique Westinghouse micarta for the handle material on this knife.

Coats' knives are sole authorship. He heat treats his own blades, and they generally test out at Rockwell sixty-one to sixty-two on his tester. He uses integral bolsters on his knives and the shields are pinned on.

"I don't have anything against the modern way of making knives with the water jet and CNC stuff, but back in 1977, when it was a big deal for me to spend eight hundred dollars on a belt grinder, I decided I wanted to do it all myself," Coats said.

Most of Coats blades are hollow ground, but, again, if a customer wants a flat ground knife, he'll do that, as well.

Coats isn't opposed to using other handle material, including elk, wood, ivory, and walrus ivory, but he doesn't use much stag these days.

"Back when I first started making knives, stag was five dollars for some really primo stuff," he said. "The price now really burns me up. If someone wants high-

end handle material, I tell them where they can order it or I ask them where they want me to get it. That solves a lot of problems in terms of cost.

"I've used a fair amount of ivory and fair amount of elk—good elk, where it has a nice white under-color to it."

Coats still make two or three fixed blades a year, but mainly he is busy making traditional pocket-knives. Houlihan said he has seen a steady improvement in Coats, knives with bigger swedges and better fit and finish.

"His early knives were well-made, totally functional, and at great prices," Houlihan said. "His knives have become more elegant, more refined, but they're still completely functional and sturdy. Any knife that Ken makes you can stick in your pocket, but I think he is making knives that are too beautiful and too collect-able to do that."

Coats credits fellow Wisconsin knife maker Ken Erickson for helping him gain a presence on knife forums on the Internet, which, along with the knife shows and word of mouth praise from customers, has helped his business grow.

"I grew up hunting and fishing with slipjoints, and I still use them," he said. "I haven't carried a knife that I haven't made for twenty years now. It was just a bonus for me that fifteen years ago, I took an interest in doing my own bone."

Ken Erickson is Driven Toward Perfection

Custom knife maker Ken Erickson is always up for a challenge when it comes to making traditional pocketknives. While Erickson does make slim, light, single-blade knives that are perfect for carrying and using, he's more than willing to make pretty much any pattern a customer wants.

Erickson's drive for perfection has already led to some additional hardware for his mantle. In 2013, Erickson won the best custom folder award at the Badger Show in Janesville, Wisconsin, with a tortoise-shell handled champagne knife after taking top honors for folders at the Blade Show a year prior with a stag-handled horseman's knife.

In a relatively short amount of time, Erickson has progressed from fixed blades to single-blade slipjoints to multi-blade slipjoints, and he has honed most of his craftsmanship through trial and error.

▲ Erickson based his horseman's knife off of one that was made in Sheffield by the company of George Wostenholm.

▲ A close up of the punch blade on the stag horseman's knife that Erickson won an award for.

Erickson lost the use of his legs after an accident and then became a gunsmith. After twenty years as a gunsmith in St. Louis, he sold his retail store and indoor shooting range and moved to Waupaca, Wisconsin but he didn't want to fully retire, so he started making fixed blades in 2002.

"I've always appreciated handmade knives," Erickson said. "I thought making knives would be something that I would really enjoy doing and that at least some of my skills as a gunsmith would carry over into making handmade knives. I became a little bored with making the fixed blades because they don't have the mechanical aspects that slipjoints have. As far as learning how to make knives, I'm mostly self-taught.

"I've read some books, including the one by Eugene Shadley and Terry Davis, and then I started poring over the knife magazines. I've never had anyone come into my shop and say 'OK, this is how we have to do things.'"

Erickson said he has learned a lot about vintage pocketknives from the old knives thread on the traditional subforum of BladeForums.com, which he said was like having an online magazine of traditional slipjoint patterns by the top companies from the turn of the century.

On the Blade Forums website, Erickson was also able to communicate with other knife makers and forge a direct relationship with his customers.

"When I first asked him to make a knife for me, I was looking at his knives and his comments on Blade Forums," said Charlie Campagna, a collector of vintage and custom traditional knives. "I was impressed with how he was seeing the correct details for the traditional-style knives. I thought to myself that here's a guy who really is seeking all of the qualities I like in the old stuff."

Campagna asked Erickson to make a custom harness jack, which some custom makers had shied away from because of the punch blade.

"I challenged him to make a knife with a punch, and he liked that," Campagna said. "He made a beautiful harness jack after I had sent him some old ones to look at. He took all of the goodness from the old ones and put it into the new one. It was really quite astounding.

"In my opinion, he's one of the very few modern makers who has that touch. You see it in Tony Bose, and you see it in Ken Erickson. They're really in tune with all of the subtle curves, beveling, and whole shape of the knife. So many modern makers build knives that are like bricks; they're well-built bricks, but they are bricks. These guys build a sculpture."

Building the harness jack represented a seachange for Erickson. He realized that he didn't want to make the same patterns over and over, and he could use his customers' knowledge to improve his craftsmanship.

"I really do enjoy pushing myself to make more complex patterns," he said. "Since I'm self-taught, a big part of that has been tapping into the knowledge of my customers, who have been heavily involved in either collecting traditional

◀ The tortoise shell scales on this congress whittler by Erickson are backed with gold foil.

▲ A stag pruner with a cap end for standing the knife up on a flat surface.

slipjoints or heavily involved in the custom end of slipjoints. I would be a fool to not take advantage of their knowledge."

Erickson is up for the challenge of making the more difficult slipjoint patterns. In addition to the horseman's and champagne knives, he's also made lockback whittlers, cattle knives, four-blade congress knives, and other complicated patterns.

Aside from Campagna, other customers have sent Erickson vintage knives to study and replicate. Instead of telling customers what patterns are available, Erickson is more than willing to work with them to build a knife that he has never made before.

Erickson also jigs his own bone. He started out buying bone that was already jigged but soon came to realize that by the time he hafted a knife, the jig-

ging didn't roll over the edges of the scales like he wanted it to.

"On a traditional slipjoint you need the jigging to have as full coverage as possible in order for it to look right," he said. "Commercial jigged bone is so flat that by the time you round the scales to meet the frame, you've lost a good portion of the jigging."

Erickson said he likes the older caramel-colored peachseed jigged bone by Schrade, but he didn't set out to copy it exactly. He uses a Dremel with cutting tools he's modified to jig the bone for his knives. Fellow Wisconsin knife maker Ken Coates helped him learn how to dye the bone.

"If I tried to shoot for an exact pattern, I don't think I could pull it off," he said. "I think everyone develops their own jigging style that is unique. I really believe the key is to have as much coverage as possible. If you look at certain commercial bone that has been put on a smaller knife, it's obvious that the jigging is too large for that size of a knife.

"I have two different jigging styles for small and larger knives. One is more elongated while the other is almost like a dimple."

As for other handle materials, Erickson has also used micarta, wood, stag, and ivory.

Erickson finishes most of his blades with a perpendicular satin finish, which he said the majority of traditional cutlers used, but he has done some knives with hand-rubbed finishes using six hundred to eight hundred grit polishes.

"I'm a fan of flat-ground blades for slipjoints," he said. "I like the blade profile that it gives you, and you can still make a really nice slicer using flat ground, provided you grind the blade thin enough to start."

While some custom knife makers have borrowed patterns from other makers, Erickson has made his own.

"I have a drawer full of patterns that I've made," Erickson said. "I'll make the pattern, both the blade and the frame, out of brass sheet first, so I can get a feel for the size of the knife, the geometry of the tang, and how all of the blades are going to lay. I don't have any spring patterns at all. I make the spring just from the way it has to fit into the frame and interact with the tang of the blade."

When asked about his goals as a knife maker, Erickson said that he wants to be known as one of the premier slipjoint knife makers, which is an elite club that some of his customers, including Campagna, already feel he has joined.

"Quite frankly, my goal is twenty or thirty years from now, or even in the present time, when guys are sitting around talking about the premier slipjoint makers, I hope my name gets mentioned," Erickson said. "I also want to help keep the quality craftsmanship alive that was available in traditional slipjoints. I want to keep that art alive. There's only way one to do that, and that's to be out there making the best knife I can.

"I don't think I'll ever achieve the perfect knife, but I'll keep trying for it. It's that pursuit of perfection that keeps driving me."

XI: Glossary

*L*ike any other hobby, the knife collecting world is chock full of terms, definitions, and phrases that new collectors may not understand at first glance. Here are a few that are common currency among knife collectors and dealers:

- Back: Also known as the spine. The top, usually unsharpened, part of a blade.
- Bail: A strong, metal half circle located on the back bolster of a knife. It can be used to attach a lanyard or string to secure it to a belt loop or other article of clothing. A lot of scout knives have bails.
- Barehead: A knife that doesn't have a cap on the end away from the blade.
- Belly: The curved section of a knife blade, usually used for skinning on hunting knives.
- Blade pick, or opener: Made by knife companies to aid in the opening of pocketknife blades, which saved wear and tear on fingernails. The blade pick was inserted into the nail nick.
- Blood groove: A misnomer for the groove or channel that runs along either side of a fixed blade knife. The correct term is fuller. Supposedly a blood groove allows blood to flow out of a wound

during a stabbing. Fullers are largely cosmetic, but practical, real-world reasons for fullers could include the lightening and strengthening of a sword blade or to allow a flat grind on a blade for easier sharpening.
- Barlow: Largely a low-cost, sturdy jack knife with long bolsters.
- Bolsters: The metal covering on the end of the knife with the blades. Earlier bolsters were made out of iron. Bolsters were also made with nickel silver (a blend of copper, zinc, and nickel also known as German steel) brass, and stainless steel. Barlow knives had longer bolsters in comparison to other patterns, which supposedly made them, stronger and better suited for hard use. Bolsters can have decorative elements, such as threaded, ribbed, grooved, rattail, and fluted designs. Bolsters also had flat facets on the outside edges or, in the case of fruit knives, were embellished with designs.
- Buffer, or buffing wheel: The bane of vintage knives' existence. Buffing wheels are used to convert vintage knife blades with patinas into bright, shiny blades that would scare off most fish. Buffing a knife blade not only removes all of a knife's

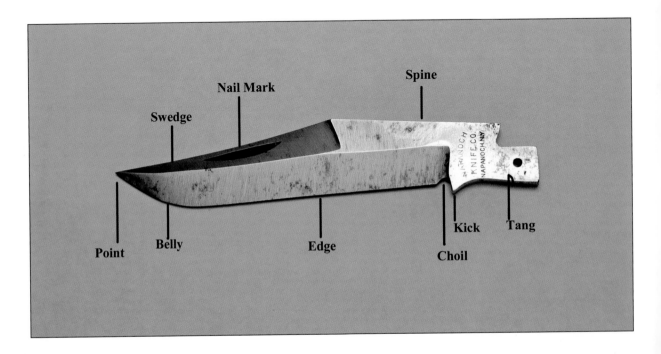

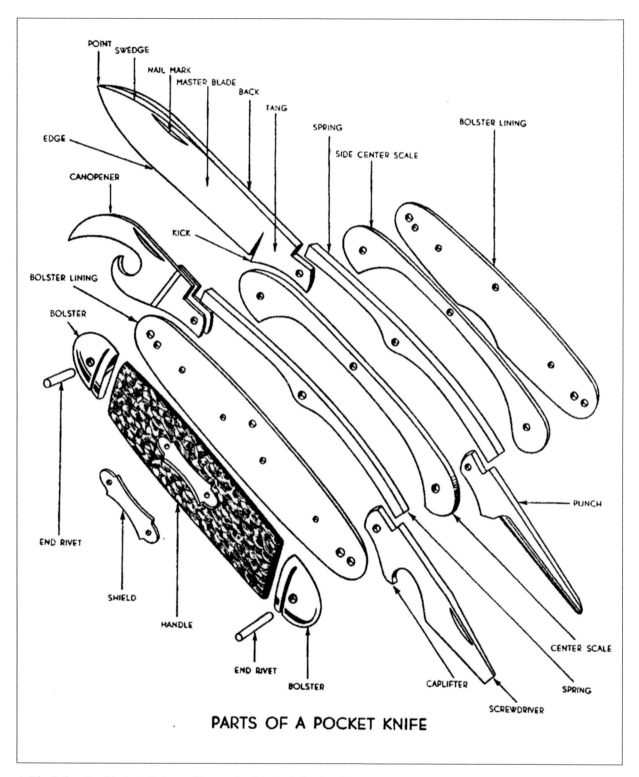

PARTS OF A POCKET KNIFE

▲ "The Cutlery Story" by Lewis D. Bement, The Associated Cutlery Industries of America, 1950.

hard-earned character, it also rounds the edges of swedges and other elements of a blade.

- Caps: The metal covering on the end of the knife that is opposite to the blades.
- Carbon: There are various types of carbon steel, but generally carbon steel was used early on by cutlery companies before the advent of stainless steel. If heat-treated correctly, most carbon steel takes an edge easily. Unlike stainless steels, carbon steels corrode more easily.
- Choil: An area on the opposite end from the tip of a blade that is cut away. On a pocketknife, a choil is located after the edge of the blade and before the tang. Its purpose is to allow sharpening of the blade along a straight surface prior to the tang.
- Clip blade: A blade with a concave curve in back of the point. Also features a cutting edge that curves upward to the tip. Narrow clip blades are also known as Turkish clips or California clips.
- Common nail mark: A short, usually crescent nail pull on a blade.
- Congress: A curved pocketknife that most commonly comes with two or four blades, although some were made with five or six blades. This American pattern always has a sheepfoot as the master blade.
- Cover: Also known as scales, the covers are the handle material of a knife, which could include jigged bone, sambar stag, celluloid, buffalo horn, wood, and mother-of-pearl.
- Crinking: A slight bending of a knife blade near the tang to allow several blades to pass each other without rubbing when opening and closing.
- Crocus: Refers to a knife blade that was finished with a polish of powdered iron oxide. Some high-end knives have a crocus, or mirror finish, on all of the blades, while others just have the mark side main blades polished with crocus.
- Drop-point blade: A blade shape that was popularized by customer maker Bob Loveless in the 1960s that was used on hunting knives.
- Eased opening: A small notch on a knife frame that allows access to a nail pull. Eased openings are generally used on multibladed knives.
- Easy opener: Also known an EZ Opener, a curved section cut out of the handle near the butt end of a blade, so the user can grab and open the blade

with his or her fingers. Easy openers were used on jack knives with large spear point blades.

- EDC: An acronym for every day carry, which is the knife a person carries on a daily basis.
- Edge: the sharpened section of a knife blade.
- False edge: The top of a blade that has been sharpened.
- Half-stop: A half-stop on a traditional pocket knife blade briefly stops a blade from fully opening due to a square-shaped tang. Blades that open without the stop are on cam, or rounded, tangs. A common myth regarding half-stops is that they provide a protective measure against a blade closing on your fingers when you are using a knife incorrectly. A better safety measure would be to use a lockback or fixed blade.
- Hardness: Today's steels are tested by the Rockwell hardness test. While harder steels hold their edges longer, getting a good edge on them can take longer. Conversely, softer steels sharpen faster but don't hold their edges as long. The ideal Rockwell hardness for knives is the upper 50s and, lower 60s range.
- Jack: A popular pattern that most commonly features two blades coming out of the same bolster. Some double-ended knives, which have a single blade on each end, are also referred to as jack knives. Jack knives come in various sizes and in a multitude of patterns.
- Jigged bone: Dyed bone, usually shin bones from cattle that have a textured process applied. Jigged bone was a less expensive alternative to stag, and some early cutlery companies referred to their jigged bone as stag bone. While there were some companies, such as Winterbottom and Rogers, that supplied jigged bone to the cutlery industry, other companies became known for their own unique jigging patterns.
- Joints: There are three types of joints on pocket-knives: sunk, half-sunk, and common joints. On premium patterns, such as penknives, the back of the blade joints were sunk to be level with the top of the handle. Knives with sunk joints keep the back of the blades from protruding when in the closed position. Half-sunk joints feature the backs of the blades just above the handle, while common joints, most often on less expensive knives,

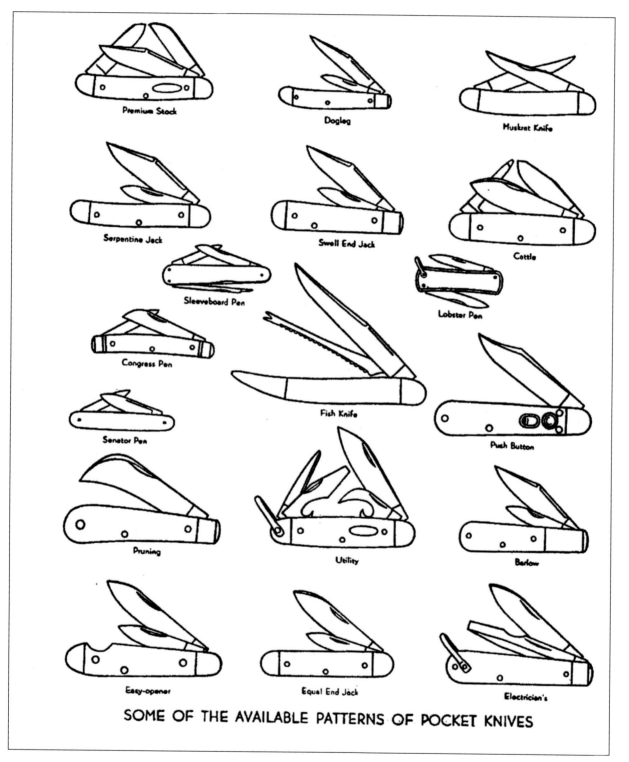

Premium Stock

Dogleg

Muskrat Knife

Serpentine Jack

Swell End Jack

Cattle

Sleeveboard Pen

Lobster Pen

Congress Pen

Senator Pen

Fish Knife

Push Button

Pruning

Utility

Barlow

Easy-opener

Equal End Jack

Electrician's

SOME OF THE AVAILABLE PATTERNS OF POCKET KNIVES

▲ "The Cutlery Story" by Lewis D. Bement, The Associated Cutlery Industries of America, 1950.

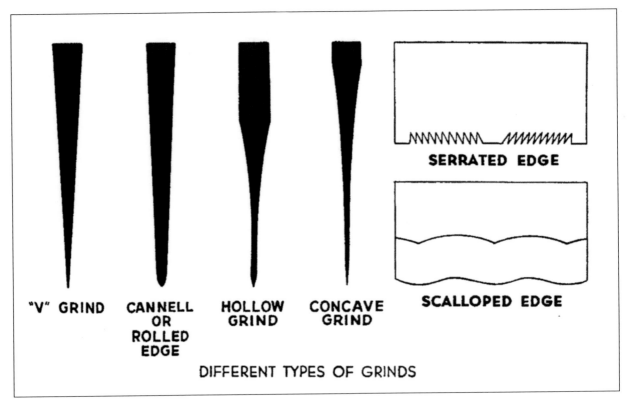

DIFFERENT TYPES OF GRINDS

"V" GRIND   CANNELL OR ROLLED EDGE   HOLLOW GRIND   CONCAVE GRIND   SERRATED EDGE   SCALLOPED EDGE

▲ The types of grinds used on fixed blades and pocketknives. "The Cutlery Story" by Lewis D. Bement, The Associated Cutlery Industries of America, 1950.

have the back of the joint sticking up out of the handle.

- Kick: A small projection at the end of the blade before the tang that keeps a blade from slamming into a spring when closed. Stovepipe kicks, which are squared off and more pronounced, were used on earlier vintage folding knives.
- Lanyard: A piece of leather or string attached to the end of a knife via a bail or lanyard hole to secure or hold a knife in place. The other end of the lanyard or thong was tied to a belt loop or clothes.
- Liner: The inside of a pocketknife frame that sits in between the handle material and blades.
- Lockback: A knife that locks into place and is released via a mechanism on the back or middle of a folding knife.
- Long pull: A long nail pull that runs from the back of the tang to the swedge of the knife. Some early pocketknives had long pulls that extended into the tangs.
- Matchstrike: A long nail pull that has fine teeth to add purchase when opening a blade. Tradition has it that some people used the matchstrike pull to strike their wooden matches against.

- Mark side: The front side of a blade with the company name and main blade nail pull. Usually a shield is located on the mark side of a knife.
- Master blade: The biggest blade in a pocketknife. The most common master blades are clip, spear, and drop-point.
- Nail pull: A groove, crescent or line, that was stamped into blades to help open them when closed. Also known as nail nicks and nail marks.
- Pen blade: A small spearpoint blade that was used to trim the end of quills prior to modern pens.
- Penknife: A small folding knife with blades—with one or more being a pen blade—at each end. Single-bladed knives are known as quill knives, but both pen and quill knives were originally used to sharpen quills for writing with ink.
- Pile side: The opposite of mark side.
- Pins: Small metal round pieces made of brass or nickel silver that were used to pin a knife together.
- Pommel: The knob on the end of a sword or knife handle.
- Ricasso: An unsharpened length of blade just above the guard or handle on a knife, dagger, sword, or bayonet.

152 • Gun Trader's Guide to Collectible Knives   www.skyhorsepublishing.com

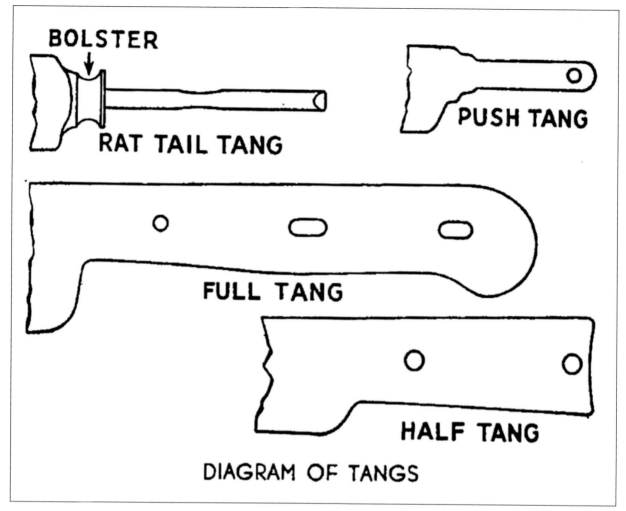

BOLSTER

RAT TAIL TANG

PUSH TANG

FULL TANG

HALF TANG

DIAGRAM OF TANGS

▲ "The Cutlery Story" by Lewis D. Bement, The Associated Cutlery Industries of America, 1950.

- Sambar: While there were other types of deer antler used, Sambar stag from India was preferred by early cutlery companies.
- Scales: Scales, or covers, are the handle parts on each side of a hunting knife or the outside parts on the sides of a pocketknife.
- Shield: Shields are decorative or trademark elements made of steel that were usually pinned into the mark-side scale of a knife after space there was inlet. There are hundreds of variations used on pocketknives, including federal, double bomb, crest, bar, curved bar, acorn, and gimp designs.
- Slip joint: A more modern term that is applied to traditional folding knives that don't lock but instead use backsprings to create the tension that keeps a knife open.
- Spacer: Material, often colorful, that is inserted between the main handle material on fixed-blade knives.
- Spring: A flat piece of steel that, when connected to the pivot pin, holds the blade open via the tension that is created. Knife blades can be mounted on a one-end spring or on two-end springs. For example, a whittler's main blade rides on two springs, while the two secondary blades ride on one spring.
- Stamps: Tang stamps on blades identify which company made the knife and, in some cases, provide information on when a knife was made. Some knives also have pattern numbers stamped on the blades.
- Square and clean: Also known, erroneously, as flush and clean. According to knife expert Bernard Levine, square and clean means that all of the edge surfaces of the tang are flush with the liners in all three positions: closed, half open and full open. The corners of the bolsters and tang are also sharp and square on these knives.

- Stainless steel: Some stainless steel knives were manufactured prior to World War I, but they became much more prevalent after World War II, namely in kitchen cutlery and utensils. While stainless does stain less than carbon, the type used for knives will rust if proper care isn't taken.
- Tang: The back part of a blade that attaches to the rest of the knife via pivot pins.
- Trapper: A specific type of jack knife that features clip and spey blades.
- Walk and talk: A term that is used to describe the action of a folding knife when it's opened or closed. A knife that has good walk and talk opens and closes smoothly with the blades snapping firmly in place in the open position.
- Whittler: A three-bladed knife with the master blade on one end and two secondary blades on the other. The master blade is provisioned on two of the springs while the secondary blades each ride on one spring. Knives with three backsprings are also called whittlers, as well as the knives that feature manicure blades as one of the secondary blades. There are numerous whittler patterns to collect.

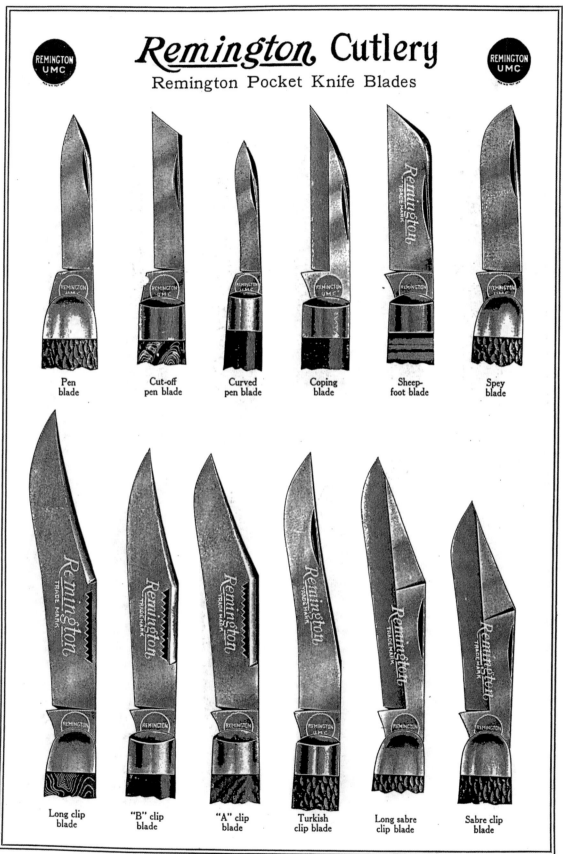

Remington Cutlery

Remington Pocket Knife Blades

Pen blade	Cut-off pen blade	Curved pen blade	Coping blade	Sheep-foot blade	Spey blade
Long clip blade	"B" clip blade	"A" clip blade	Turkish clip blade	Long sabre clip blade	Sabre clip blade

"The Prime Function of a Knife is to Cut—to Cut Keenly"—Remington

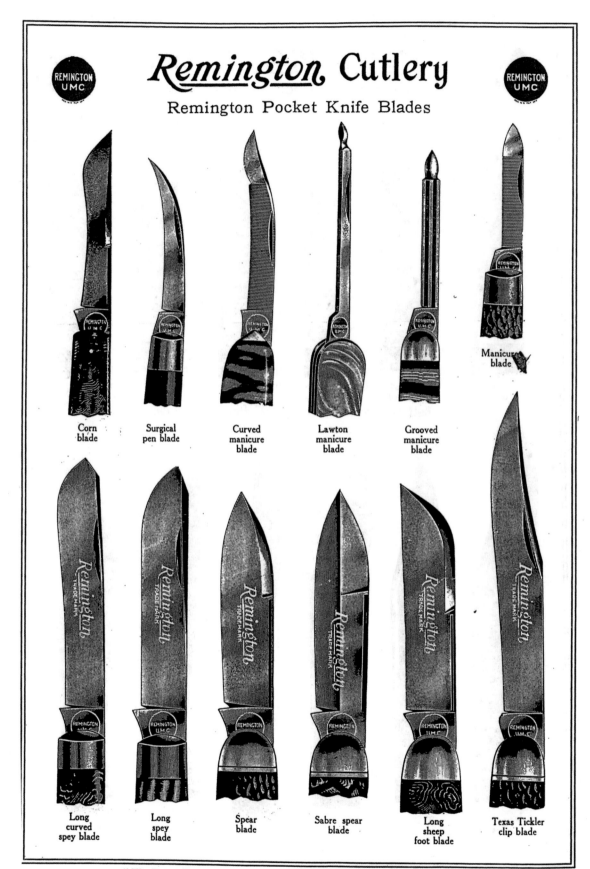

Remington Cutlery

Remington Pocket Knife Blades

Corn blade

Surgical pen blade

Curved manicure blade

Lawton manicure blade

Grooved manicure blade

Manicure blade

Long curved spey blade

Long spey blade

Spear blade

Sabre spear blade

Long sheep foot blade

Texas Tickler clip blade

"The Prime Function of a Knife is to Cut—to Cut Keen." Remington

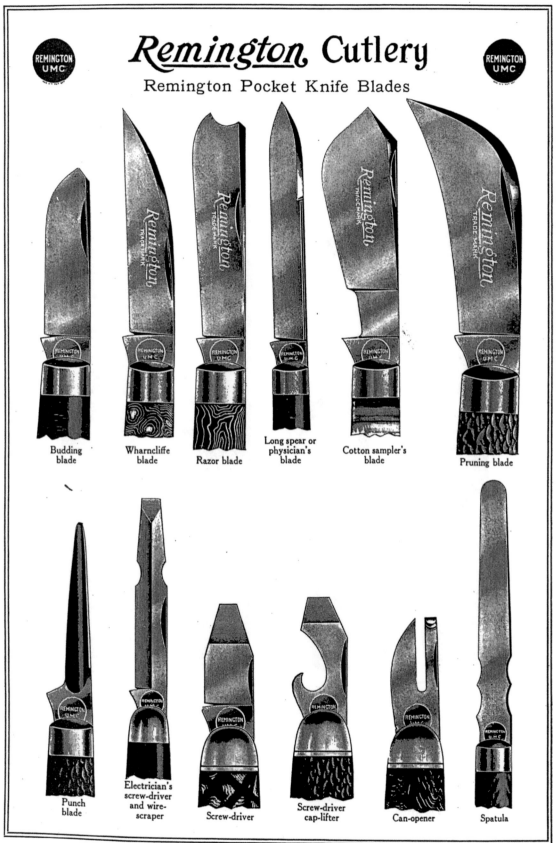

Remington Cutlery

Remington Pocket Knife Blades

Budding blade	Wharncliffe blade	Razor blade	Long spear or physician's blade	Cotton sampler's blade	Pruning blade

Punch blade	Electrician's screw-driver and wire-scraper	Screw-driver	Screw-driver cap-lifter	Can-opener	Spatula

"The Prime Function of a Knife is to Cut—to Cut Keenly"—Remington

On the Net

Joining a forum is one way of finding out more about knife collecting. Here are a few online knife forums and other resource websites:

Allaboutpocketknives.com
Bladeforums.com
Britishblades.com
Knifedogs.com
knife-expert.com
Knifeforums.com
iknifecollector.com
usualsuspect.net

◀ Pictured are screenshots of three of the websites you can visit to learn about knife collecting.

Acknowledgments

nyone who writes about history stands on the shoulders of others, and in my case there have been many shoulders to stand on over the years. Special thanks to Tony Bose, Kerry Hampton, and Bernard Levine for answering numerous questions, checking the content (although any and all of the mistakes are my own), and providing help with the pictures. Hampton also wrote the chapter on swedges and took the pictures.

I literally could not have assembled all of the knife pictures without the help of the following: Rick Menefee, Alan Dodge, Ken Erickson, Charlie Campagna, Ken Coats, John Ferguson, Charles Lamb, Barry Wolder, and Arthur Green. Neal Punchard and Michael Critchlow also chipped in by writing the chapter on Solingen and Sheffield respectively, and helped out with other pictures, as well. Barry Johnson provided the photos of the Oregon Knife Show. My heartfelt thanks to all of the above.

The two books that I rely on the most are *Levine's Guide to Knives and their Values, Fourth Edition* and *Goin's Encyclopedia of Cutlery Markings*. *Joseph Smith's Key to Manufactories of Sheffield* is worth picking up if you can find a copy. A subscription to *Knife World* will also go a long way toward increasing your knowledge about fixed blades and folding pocketknives.

The line drawings and other illustrations, unless otherwise noted, came from out-of-date knife catalogues or pamphlets.

Index